RICH TRADITIONS

RICH TRAD

Scrap

ITIONS
Quilts to Paper Piece

NANCY MAHONEY

Martingale™
& COMPANY

CREDITS

President: *Nancy J. Martin*
CEO: *Daniel J. Martin*
Publisher: *Jane Hamada*
Editorial Director: *Mary V. Green*
Managing Editor: *Tina Cook*
Technical Editor: *Ursula Reikes*
Copy Editor: *Karen Koll*
Design Director: *Stan Green*
Illustrator: *Laurel Strand*
Cover Designer: *Stan Green*
Text Designer: *Trina Stahl*
Photographer: *Brent Kane*

Rich Traditions: Scrap Quilts to Paper Piece
© 2002 by Nancy Mahoney

That Patchwork Place® is an imprint
of Martingale & Company™.

Martingale & Company
20205 144th Avenue NE
Woodinville, WA 98072-8478
www.martingale-pub.com

Printed in Hong Kong
07 06 05 04 03 02   8 7 6 5 4 3 2 1

Library of Congress Cataloging-in-Publication data is available upon request.
ISBN 1-56477-425-2

MISSION STATEMENT

We are dedicated to providing quality products and service by working together to inspire creativity and to enrich the lives we touch.

DEDICATION

To my mother, Catherine Elizabeth Ochsner Price, who taught me to love books. She would have been very pleased. And to Tom Reichert, my partner and best friend, whose love, guidance, patience, and support have made many things possible over the years.

ACKNOWLEDGMENTS

There are many people who supported and encouraged me in various ways while I was writing this book. I wish to extend a special thanks to the following:

David Peha, owner of Fabric Sales Company, for his support, understanding, and friendship.

Gretchen Engle, Barbara Ford, Sue Lohse, and Lea Wang, who are wonderful machine quilters. I could not have accomplished this book without their help, and I can't thank them enough.

Cheryl Little from the Cotton Club, Sandy Muckenthaler from Hoffman Fabrics, and Susan Ellis from Quilts & Other Comforts for helping to search for fabrics.

Clothworks, Hoffman Fabrics, R. J. R. Fabrics, and P & B Textiles, who have been very generous with their fabrics.

Nancy Lee Chong, for the generous use of her Autumn Leaves block.

Ursula Reikes, my editor, for all her help and her outstanding editing job.

Nancy Martin, Mary Green, and the staff at Martingale & Company for their hard work, encouragement, and support. Thank you for the opportunity to share my quilts.

CONTENTS

INTRODUCTION

SOME QUILTMAKERS think that a scrap quilt must be made using a large number of different fabrics, often a set number. My definition is a little more liberal. I feel that any quilt containing a variety of fabrics is a scrap quilt. This book will show you how to use your scraps and stacks of fat quarters in different ways to make scrap quilts. You can, of course, make a quilt using many different colors and fabrics, as in "Pineapple Splash" (page 68). But you can also limit the colors and fabrics—to just blues and whites, for example, as in "Blue Moon" (page 49). Both quilts are scrap quilts.

All of the quilts in this book except "Autumn Leaves" (page 65) are made from paper-pieced versions of traditional blocks that quilters have been using for generations. Piecing on a paper foundation gives you greater accuracy and precision than does traditional piecing. Paper piecing is particularly great for blocks with lots of pieces or very small pieces. "Pineapple Splash" (page 68) is a good example of a quilt that would be difficult to make without paper piecing.

Many of the quilts feature a side-by-side setting. Exciting and surprising secondary designs come to life as the individual boundaries of blocks disappear and an overall design emerges.

So, if you love scrap quilts and traditional blocks, now is the time to grab your scrap basket and start stitching.

I liked assorting those little figured bits of cotton cloth, for they were scraps of gowns I had seen worn, and they reminded me of the persons who wore them. . . . One fragment, in particular, was like a picture to me. It was a delicate pink and brown sea-moss pattern, on a white ground, a piece of a dress belonging to my married sister, who was to me bride and angel in one.

—LUCY LARCOM
A New England Girlhood: Outlined from Memory

QUILTMAKING BASICS

GLOSSARY OF TERMS

COLOR FAMILY: A catagory comprised of fabrics that are the same color but have different values, textures, scale, and intensity.

CONTRAST: Differences evident among two or more fabrics placed side by side.

INTENSITY: The strength or brightness of a color.

MONOCHROMATIC: From one color family.

SCALE: The relative size of the motif in printed fabrics.

VALUE: The lightness or darkness of a fabric.

VISUAL TEXTURE: The pattern printed on a fabric.

FABRIC SELECTION

I LOVE SCRAP quilts; they are my favorite quilts to make. When I look at a scrap quilt, the fabrics are memories of other quilts and occasions. Today's scraps become tomorrow's quilts.

Much has been written about selecting fabrics for a scrap quilt, but I get bogged down trying to follow the rules. The problem with rules is that I can generally find an exception to each one. So rather than give you a set of rules, I have provided some guidelines and four fabric recipes that I have found helpful in making scrap quilts.

Start by looking at lots of scrap quilts, vintage as well as new, in books and at quilt shows. Make note of what you like and of what you think doesn't work well. Then consider the following guidelines, and the fabric recipes starting on page 12, as you make choices about color and fabrics.

- Always use 100 percent–cotton fabrics for the best results.

- Choose colors according to value. The lightness or darkness of a color is more important than the color itself. If your quilt seems lifeless, it probably needs more contrast. Add a color that is lighter or darker or brighter.

- Stretch the range of colors within a color group. "Red" can include everything from rusty brown to scarlet to reddish purple.

- Fabrics that vary in intensity can add dimension to your quilt. The more intense colors will stand out and advance toward the viewer. Bright, clear colors are high in intensity; dull or grayed colors are low in intensity.

- Use a variety of scales and textures to make your quilt interesting. Florals, plaids, stripes, and geometric designs in different scales can all work together in a quilt.

- Try including a few novelty prints to add a little surprise for the viewer. These prints are often not noticed when viewed from a distance. Only upon closer inspection will you see them.

- Don't scrutinize each print too carefully. Think of blending the fabrics instead of matching them exactly. Scrap quilts are more intriguing if the fabrics aren't too closely coordinated.

- Add neutral colors, such as white, beige, cream, gray, or even black to give your eyes a place to rest. Cream or white will make the design look crisp or clean. Black will make the other colors glow.

FABRIC RECIPES

THE FOUR FABRIC recipes described in the following sections are simple recipes that you can follow to choose colors for your quilt. As you choose fabrics, refer to the above guidelines. Remember, for any of the recipes to be successful, you need to use a variety of prints that vary in value, intensity, scale, and texture.

Crazy Scrap Recipe

A crazy scrap recipe is just what it sounds like. It's crazy and accommodates any color, so the sky's the limit. This is a fun scrap quilt to make, but planning it can be intimidating. Don't try to coordinate fabrics for the whole quilt. Instead, try

choosing colors for one block at a time. When you finish a block, place it on your design wall. Then begin your next block, choosing colors that are compatible with neighboring blocks; don't worry about the color of blocks that are farther away.

- The blocks in "Pineapple Splash" (page 68 and below) were made using a different fabric in each position within a block. The fabrics are repeated in other blocks throughout the quilt.

- I did have one rule for "Confetti" (page 42 and below): all the fabrics had to be batiks. I selected two light and two dark fabrics for each block.

- "Cinnamon and Spice" (page 45), "Spoolin' Around" (page 39), and "T-Time" (page 36) use a different light and dark fabric in each block. The light fabrics minimize the conflict between the colors in neighboring blocks.

Limited Scrap Recipe

A limited scrap recipe is more restrictive than the crazy scrap recipe because colors are placed in specific positions within the block or quilt. If quilts made with a crazy scrap recipe are too intimidating or flamboyant for you, start with a limited-scrap-recipe quilt. Your quilt will still look scrappy, but your fabric choices will be more controlled. For a more unified look, try using a common background or a neutral color.

- "Autumn Leaves" (page 65 and below) uses a limited number of fabrics for the leaves and different black tone-on-tones for the background. The autumn-themed colors make the leaves look like they have fallen from a tree, and the black background prints unify. Notice that the black background is also used in the sashing and inner border, giving the illusion that the leaves are floating.

- "Twist and Shout" (page 59 and below) is made entirely from batik fabrics, including the black background. The jewel-tone fabrics are limited to four different fabrics within each color. The black batik used for the background unifies the quilt. A similarly striking effect could be achieved with a different set of fabrics and a light background.

- "Garden Path" (page 30) has both a limited color palette and specific color placement. The quilt features three colors, although a wide range of values is used within each color. The reds range from a dark red to a brighter red-orange. The yellows range from light to dark. Even the black prints vary in value and texture. The reds, yellows, and blacks are used in the same position in each block.

- Like "Garden Path," "Pineapple Express" (page 33) also has a limited color palette and specific color placement. The reds, yellows, and blacks are used in the same position in each block. Various light-value prints are used for the background. Consistent color placement creates the design structure and has a calming effect.

Two-Color Recipe

In a two-color recipe, all of the fabrics except the background fabric are from the same color family, which means they are the same color but have different values, textures, scales, and intensities. The two-color recipe is also sometimes called monochromatic, because there is just one nonbackground color used. Quilts using this recipe can be very dramatic. Limiting the colors doesn't mean you need to limit the fabrics. With this recipe, think in terms of blending fabrics.

- "Blue Moon" (page 49 and below) uses a variety of blue prints and a range of off-white-to-cream prints with small blue motifs. The overall effect is less contrast between the background prints and the blue prints. The simple side-by-side setting creates a strong design.

- "Tequila Sunrise" (page 79) uses a variety of red prints. Notice how the lighter and brighter prints add life to the quilt. The high contrast between the red spikes and the light background makes the quilt seem to vibrate and glow.
- "Optical Fibers" (page 52) is primarily a two-color quilt, with one additional color thrown in as an accent. A variety of purple and yellow prints are used for the blocks. A third color, green, is found in the pieced border.

- "Red Chili Peppers" (page 71 and below) is a two-color quilt made with red and black. Red prints are used in the melon centers of the blocks and red points in the arcs. Black tone-on-tone prints are used for the black points in the arcs. Red-and-black prints are used in the corners of each block, sashing, and outer borders. The overall effect of "Red Chili Peppers" is busier than the other two-color quilts because the red-and-black prints are medium to large scale. The prints also have a higher contrast than the tone-on-tone prints used in the other quilts in this category.

Theme-Print Recipe

A theme-print recipe is based on one fabric, usually a large-scale print that is used in the blocks and in the border. It is one of the easiest scrap quilts to make. Choosing colors for the quilt is simple because the colors for the other fabrics in the quilt are based on the colors in the theme print. Remember—although the colors may be limited, the fabrics still need to vary in value, intensity, scale, and texture.

- "Swimming Upstream" (page 62 and below) was inspired by a large-scale fish print. Various gold and navy prints are used along with the fish print in the blocks. Because an inner border is not used to separate the blocks from the outer border, the blocks appear to float on the fish print.

- "Peony Star" (page 75) uses a floral theme print. A variety of green and red prints are used for the blocks. A variety of light prints are used for the background.
- "Crossing the Blues" (page 56) uses a large-scale green print that contains a little yellow and blue. Yellow and blue prints are combined with the large-scale green print in the blocks.

MAKING SAMPLE BLOCKS

ONCE YOU'VE DECIDED on a color scheme and picked your fabrics, it's a good idea to make four sample blocks to test your color choices on a small scale before making all the blocks for your quilt. Put the four blocks on a vertical design wall and analyze the results. Do you like the way the colors look together? If you don't like a block, reject it and make another one. You can always use the reject on the back of the quilt. If a fabric isn't working, simply substitute another one before making the rest of the blocks. When you're satisfied with the sample blocks, you can continue making blocks with the confidence that the colors will work together just as you planned.

As you complete blocks, place them on the design wall. This lets you view them from a distance. When all the blocks are completed, rearrange them as needed to achieve a balanced design of color and texture.

As with most things, selecting fabrics and colors takes a little practice. Your confidence in your decisions will improve with each quilt you make. Most of all, have fun; a scrap quilt can be your chance to go wild.

FAT QUARTERS AND FAT EIGHTHS

Fat quarters (18" x 21") or fat eighths (9" x 21") are a great way to add fabrics to your stash, and they are the perfect size for scrap quilts. Look for these wonderful little bundles in baskets or bins at your local quilt shop or fabric store.

NOTE: *I also purchase precut squares in a variety of sizes from catalogs and quilt clubs. This allows me to add to my stash small pieces of fabrics that I might not buy otherwise.*

The blocks in this book can all be made with a fat quarter or less of each print, with the exception of theme prints. Each quilt plan indicates the total amount of assorted fabrics needed for each color. The actual amount needed of each print will vary depending on the number of fabrics you decide to use. For example, the quilt plan for "Spoolin' Around" on page 39 indicates 1¼ yards total of assorted multicolored prints. However, each block uses a different print, so the amount needed of each print is less than a fat eighth.

PAPER PIECING

PAPER PIECING IS a method of block or unit construction in which strips or cut pieces of fabric are sewn to a paper foundation in numerical order. The paper stabilizes the fabric so that you don't need to worry too much about the grain of the fabric, except for those pieces that are on the outside edges of the block. I do try to cut these so that the edges are on the straight grain.

Paper piecing requires more fabric than other methods, but the scraps can be used to create other scrap quilts.

Copying the Paper Foundations

You will need one paper foundation pattern for each block. Make all the copies for the quilt project on the same copy machine. Check to make sure the shapes are not distorted before making all the copies. Use lightweight copy paper or paper made specifically for foundations, such as *Papers for Foundation Piecing* available from Martingale & Company.

Cutting Fabric for Paper Piecing

The instructions for each quilt include a cutting list that indicates how to cut the pieces for blocks and where the pieces will be used. When cut as directed, all pieces are large enough to cover the intended area on the paper foundation plus seam allowances. Two symbols are used to indicate when to cut squares into half-square triangles or quarter-square triangles. When you see this symbol, ◹, cut the squares once diagonally to make half-square triangles.

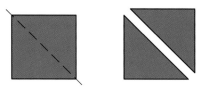

When you see this symbol, ⊠, cut the squares twice diagonally to make quarter-square triangles.

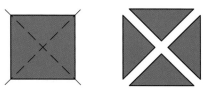

About Paper Piecing

Before you begin paper piecing, consider the following important points:

- The block design printed on the paper foundation is the reverse of the finished block. If you desire specific color placement, make a fabric mock-up of your finished block or use colored pencils to color in the areas as a reminder of the color placement.

- After photocopying the block design, trim the paper foundation ¼" from the cutting line. This makes the paper foundation easier to maneuver under the presser foot. Also, if the fabric pieces extend beyond the paper foundation, you know the pieces are large enough to allow for the seam allowance around the outer edges.

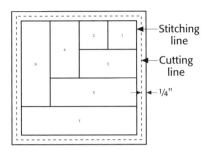

- Set your stitch length to a shorter than usual setting, 13 to 15 stitches per inch. The shorter stitch makes paper removal easier. If the stitches are shorter than 15 stitches per inch, however, they are very difficult to remove should you need to undo a seam.

- Stitch on the printed side of the paper foundation and sew exactly on the line. Begin stitching every seam at least ¼" before the seam line and finish ¼" beyond the seam line.

- After sewing each fabric piece, trim the seam allowance to ¼". Press the seam after each fabric is added. Otherwise, you may get a tuck in the fabric and the patches will not be the correct size.

TIP: *Use a scrap of muslin to protect your pressing surface from any toner that may transfer from the photocopies when pressing the blocks.*

- After the block is finished, use a ruler to trim the outer edges to the exact size, including a ¼" seam allowance. Do not stitch around the paper foundation perimeter; this will make removing the paper very difficult.

- Remove the paper before sewing the units and blocks together.

Paper Piecing the Blocks

The blocks in this book fall into two categories—those that use long strips, and those that use cut pieces of fabric. The instructions for each quilt indicate whether or not the strips are cut into smaller pieces. Blocks made with long strips are Quarter Log Cabin, Pickle Dish, Blazing Star, and New York Beauty. All of the other blocks are made with cut pieces.

Blocks Made with Long Strips

1. With the blank side of the paper up, position the fabric for piece 1 right side up to cover area 1 plus a generous seam allowance. Turn the paper and fabric over, being careful not to move the fabric, and pin in place on the marked side of the paper.

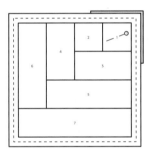

2. Place a strip of fabric for piece 2 on top of piece 1, right sides together. Make sure the fabric extends beyond the sewing line for the seam allowance.

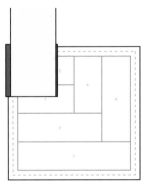

3. Hold the layers in place and carefully position the unit under the presser foot, paper side up. Sew on the line between areas 1 and 2, starting ¼" before the line and extending ¼" beyond.

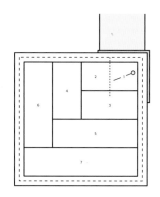

4. Trim the excess part of piece 2.

5. Fold the paper back to reveal the seam allowance. Place a ruler along the edge of the paper and trim the seam allowance to ¼".

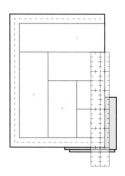

6. Open piece 2 and press the seam with a dry iron. Do not use steam.

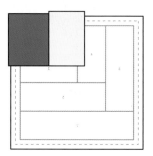

7. Repeat steps 2–6 to add piece 3.

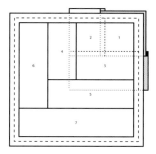

8. Continue adding pieces in numerical order until all the pieces have been sewn to the paper foundation.

9. With a ruler, cut on the outside cutting line.

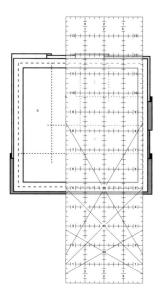

10. Remove the paper before sewing the units and blocks together.

Blocks Made with Cut Pieces

1. With the blank side of the paper up, position the fabric for piece 1 right side up to cover area 1 plus a generous seam allowance. Turn the paper and fabric over, being careful not to

move the fabric, and pin the fabric in place through the marked side of the paper.

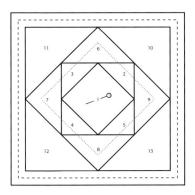

2. Place a cut piece of fabric for piece 2 on top of piece 1, right sides together. Make sure the fabric extends beyond the sewing line for the seam allowance.

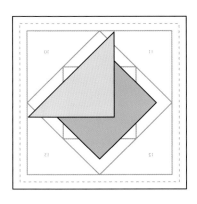

3. Hold the layers in place and carefully position the unit under the presser foot, paper side up. Sew on the line between areas 1 and 2, starting ¼" before the line and extending ¼" beyond.

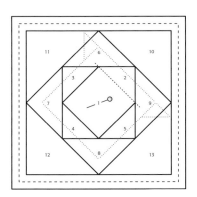

4. Fold the paper back to reveal the seam allowance. Place a ruler along the edge of the paper and trim the seam allowance to ¼".

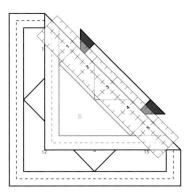

5. Open the piece and press the seam with a dry iron. Do not use steam.

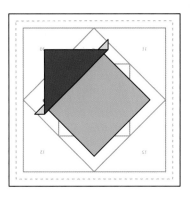

6. Trim any excess fabric if necessary.

7. Repeat steps 2–6 to add piece 3.

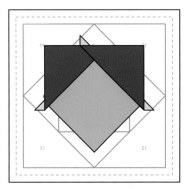

8. Continue adding pieces in numerical order until all the pieces have been sewn to the paper foundation.

9. With a ruler, cut along the outside cutting line.

10. Remove the paper before sewing the units and blocks together.

JOINING CURVED UNITS

THREE BLOCKS—Blazing Star, New York Beauty, and Pickle Dish—are made of units with curved pieces. Joining the units is not difficult; it just requires lots of pinning and a little easing. Follow these basic steps to piece any of the curved pieces in this book.

1. Paper piece the units for the block you are making. Fold the pieces in half and mark the center of each with a pin.

2. Pin the pieces together at the centers and at both ends. Then pin the rest of the seam, easing the pieces together as needed.

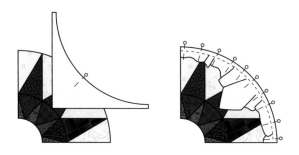

BLAZING STAR

PICKLE DISH

NEW YORK BEAUTY

3. With a ¼"-wide seam allowance, sew slowly along the curved edge.

4. Press the seam as indicated by the pressing arrow.

JOINING THE BLOCKS

WHEN YOU'VE COMPLETED all the blocks for your quilt, it's time to sew them together. Be sure to remove the paper from the blocks before joining them. Arrange the blocks in rows, referring to the color photo and illustrations of the quilt. For side-by-side setting, arrange the blocks in horizontal and vertical rows. Sew the blocks together in horizontal rows with ¼" seam allowances; then join the rows. Press the seams as indicated by the pressing arrows.

For on-point settings, arrange the blocks in diagonal rows. Sew the blocks and side triangles together in diagonal rows. Then join the rows and add the corner triangles last. Press the seams as indicated by the pressing arrows.

BORDERS WITH STRAIGHT-CUT CORNERS

ALL OF THE quilts in this book have borders with straight-cut corners. "Cinnamon and Spice" (page 45) and "Tequila Sunrise" (page 79) also have pieced borders. Yardage requirements for narrow borders (those less than 2" wide) are based on cutting strips across the width of the fabric and piecing the strips with a diagonal seam if necessary. This is the most fabric-efficient way to cut border strips. However, I prefer to cut border strips from the lengthwise grain of the fabric. Although this does require more fabric, seaming is not necessary to achieve the correct length. When applicable, there is a note following the materials list indicating the amount to buy for narrow borders if you prefer to cut strips on the lengthwise grain.

Joining Crosswise Strips with a Diagonal Seam

To join crosswise-grain strips with a diagonal seam, sew the ends of the strips at right angles with right sides together. Stitch across the diagonal and trim ¼" from the seam line. Join all strips end to end to make one long continuous strip. Then measure, trim borders from the long strip, and attach as directed.

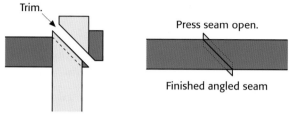

Piecing Border Strips

Adding a Border Element

When I don't have enough fabric to cut strips on the lengthwise grain, I will cut strips on the crosswise grain. Instead of joining two strips to achieve the required length, I like to add an element, like a square, to join the strips. I cut these elements from a close, but different, fabric. The resulting border strip looks like it is made from one fabric, but when viewed up close, it reveals the surprise square. The yellow inner border in "Confetti" (page 42) and the red inner border in "Garden Path" (page 30) both have this additional border element.

To make a border with an added square, cut two strips from the crosswise grain in the required width for each side of the quilt. Cut one square the same size as the strip width. For example, if you cut 2"-wide strips, then cut a 2" x 2" square. You could also add a rectangle to join two strips.

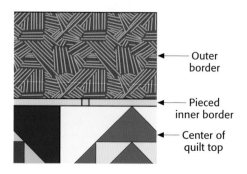

← Outer border

← Pieced inner border

← Center of quilt top

If your quilt is extremely large, you may need to cut three strips for each side and join the strips with two elements. I've made a note in the quilt directions when I used this technique to piece a border.

GARDEN PATH
A small square links strips in the red border.

CONFETTI
From a distance, the yellow border looks like a single strip of fabric, but closer scrutiny reveals a joining square.

Adding Borders

Measurements for border strips are provided in the cutting directions for each quilt. These measurements include about 2" extra because I like to cut border strips a little bigger and then trim them to the actual size of the quilt. If you are joining strips with a diagonal seam, make one long continuous strip and then cut strips as indicated.

1. Cut 2 strips for the side length as indicated in the pattern, joining strips as needed. Lay the strips on the center of the quilt top from top to bottom and trim the ends to fit the quilt top. Mark the center of the border strips and the quilt top. Attach 1 strip to each side, pinning at each end of the strip and then matching and pinning the centers. Ease any fullness as you pin the rest of each strip. Sew each strip and press the seams toward the border.

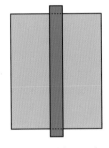

Trimming Side Borders

2. Cut 2 strips for the top and bottom as indicated in the pattern, joining strips as needed. Lay the strips on the center of the quilt top from side to side, including the side borders, and trim the ends to fit the quilt top. Mark the center of the border strips and the quilt top. Attach 1 strip to the top, pinning at each end of the strip and then matching and pinning the centers. Ease any fullness as you pin the rest of the strip. Repeat for the bottom strip. Sew each strip and press the seams toward the border.

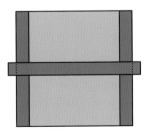

Trimming Top and
Bottom Borders

LAYERING THE QUILT

THE QUILT SANDWICH consists of the backing, batting, and quilt top. Cut the quilt backing 4" larger than the quilt top all the way around. For quilts larger than 40", you will need to piece the backing. The seam can run horizontally or vertically, unless the fabric is a print that is best viewed from a specific direction. When piecing the backing, trim the selvages before sewing the pieces together. Press the seams open to reduce bulk.

When the backing is just a little too narrow for the quilt top, you can solve the problem with a little creative piecing. Some methods take more time than others, but pieced backs are fun to make and another way to use scraps.

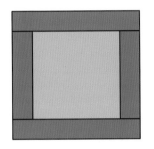

Center Square
with Border Strips

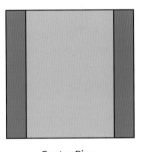

Center Piece
with Border Strips
on Each Side

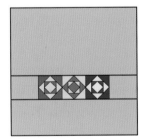

Backing Pieced Using
Leftover Blocks
Blocks can be placed
vertically or horizontally.

You can also piece together leftover scraps of fabric to create a backing large enough for your quilt top. This is most effective when you use the same fabrics that are used in the front of the quilt top. The following example shows a variety of same-size squares sewn together, but you could also sew together pieces of varying sizes.

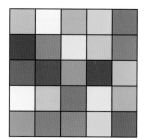

You can buy batting by the yard or purchase it packaged in standard bed sizes. Select a thin batting for hand or machine quilting. Cut the batting at least 4" larger than the quilt top.

To put it all together:

1. Spread the backing, wrong side up, on a flat, clean surface. Anchor it with pins or masking tape. Be careful not to stretch the backing out of shape.

2. Spread the batting over the backing, smoothing out any wrinkles.

3. Place the pressed quilt top, right side up, on top of the batting. Smooth out any wrinkles and make sure the edges of the quilt top are parallel to the edges of the backing.

4. Starting in the center, baste with needle and thread and work diagonally to each corner. Continue basting in a grid of horizontal and vertical lines 6" to 8" apart. Finish by basting

around the edges, about ⅛" from the edge of the quilt top.

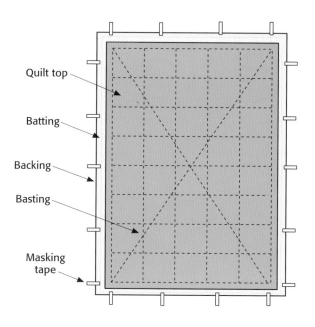

For machine quilting, you may baste the layers with #2 rustproof safety pins. Place pins about 6" to 8" apart, away from the areas you intend to quilt.

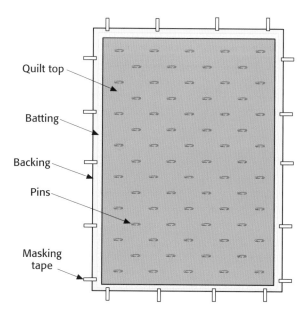

QUILTING TECHNIQUES

Hand Quilting

To quilt by hand, you will need short, sturdy needles (called "Betweens"), quilting thread, and a thimble to fit the middle finger of your sewing hand. Most quilters use a frame or hoop to support their work. Use the smallest needle you can comfortably handle; the finer the needle, the smaller your stitches will be.

1. Thread your needle with a single strand of quilting thread about 18" long. Make a small knot and insert the needle in the top layer about 1" from the point where you want to start stitching. Pull the needle out at the point where quilting will begin and gently pull the thread until the knot pops through the fabric and into the batting.

2. Take small, evenly spaced stitches through all 3 layers. Rock the needle up and down until you have 3 or 4 stitches on the needle.

3. To end a line of quilting, make a small knot close to the last stitch; then backstitch, running the thread a needle's length through the batting. Gently pull the thread until the knot pops into the batting; clip the thread at the quilt's surface.

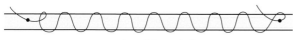

Hand-Quilting Stitch

Machine Quilting

Machine quilting is suitable for all types and sizes of quilts and allows you to complete a quilt quickly.

For straight-line quilting, it is extremely helpful to have a walking foot to help feed the layers through the machine without shifting or puckering. Some machines have a built-in walking foot; other machines require a separate attachment. The two most common forms of straight-line quilting are quilting in the ditch and outline quilting.

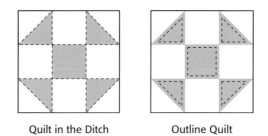

Quilt in the Ditch   Outline Quilt

For free-motion quilting, you need a darning foot and the ability to drop the feed dogs on your machine. With free-motion quilting, you do not turn the fabric under the needle but instead guide the fabric in the direction of the design. Because the feed dogs are lowered, the stitch length is determined by the speed at which you run the machine and feed the fabric under the foot. Use free-motion quilting to outline a quilt pattern in the fabric or to create stippling and many other designs.

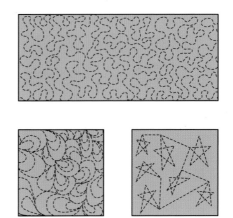

Free-motion quilting may feel awkward at first, so it's a good idea to practice on a layer of fabric scraps until you get the feel of moving the fabric with your hands and controlling the speed to get even stitches.

Straight-line Quilting

Squaring Up the Quilt

WHEN THE QUILTING is completed, it will be necessary to square up your quilt before sewing on the binding. Align a ruler with the seam line of

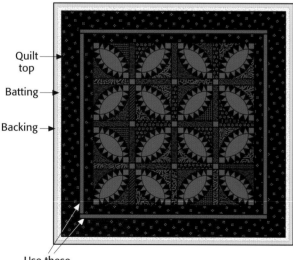

Quilt top

Batting

Backing

Use these seam lines as a guide.

the outer border and measure the width of the border in several places. Using the narrowest measurement, position a ruler along the seam line of the outer border and trim the excess batting and backing from all four sides. At each corner, use a large square ruler to square up the corners.

Binding

I THINK OF the binding as the last chance to add to the overall look of the quilt. If you want the binding to disappear, then use the same fabric for the binding and the outer border. "Twist and Shout" (page 59) and "Crossing the Blues" (page 56) both use the same fabric for the border and binding.

If you want the binding to be noticed, use a different fabric than the one used in the outer border. It could be the same fabric that was used for an inner border, as in "Peony Star" (page 75), or one of the fabrics used in the blocks, as in "Swimming Upstream" (page 62). The binding can also be made from leftover strips, provided the strips are the correct width or can be cut down to the desired width. "Pineapple Express" (page 33) has a binding made from thirteen different fabrics. Whatever you choose, it should complement the quilt top.

I prefer a double-fold binding cut on the straight grain. A straight-grain binding is easier to work with and takes less fabric than a bias-cut binding. You will need enough strips to go around the perimeter of the quilt plus about 10" for seams and turning corners. The number of strips to cut is specified for each quilt. If you are going to attach a sleeve to the back of your quilt for hanging, turn to "Adding a Sleeve" on page 28 and attach it now, before you bind the edges.

I cut 2"-wide strips for my binding. This makes a narrow, tight binding. Depending on your batting choice, you may want to cut the strips wider.

1. Cut 2"-wide strips across the width of the fabric as required for your quilt.

2. Join the strips at right angles and stitch across the corner. Trim the excess fabric, leaving a ¼" seam allowance, and press the seam open.

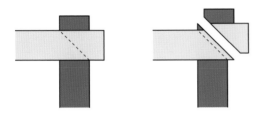

3. Fold the binding in half lengthwise, wrong sides together, and press.

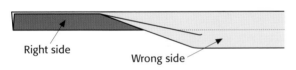

Right side

Wrong side

4. Unfold the binding at one end. Cut end at a 45° angle and fold over ¼".

Fold line

5. Starting on the bottom edge of the quilt, stitch the binding to the quilt with a ¼" seam allowance. Begin stitching 3" from the start of the binding. Stop stitching ¼" from the corner and backstitch.

Quilt top

¼"

Binding strip

6. Remove the quilt from the sewing machine. Fold the binding up and away from the quilt, and then down to create an angled pleat at the corner.

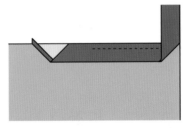

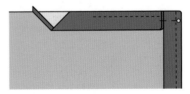

7. Start stitching at the fold of the binding. Backstitch at the beginning of the seam and then continue stitching along the edge of the quilt top. Stop ¼" from the corner and backstitch. Repeat step 6 to form the mitered corner. Continue stitching around the quilt, repeating the mitering process at each corner.

8. When you reach the beginning of the binding, stop 3" from where you started and backstitch. Remove the quilt from the machine. Trim the end 1" longer than needed and tuck the end inside the beginning strip. Pin in place, making sure the strip lies flat. Stitch the rest of the binding.

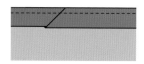

9. Turn the binding to the back of the quilt. Hand stitch in place with the folded edge covering the row of machine stitching. At each corner, fold the binding to form a miter on the back of the quilt.

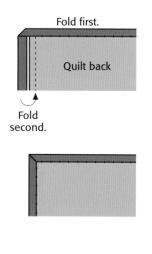

Fold first.

Quilt back

Fold second.

ADDING A SLEEVE

IF YOU PLAN to hang your quilt, attach a sleeve or rod pocket to the back before attaching the binding. From the leftover backing fabric, cut an 8"-wide strip of fabric equal to the width of your quilt. You may need to piece two or three strips together for larger quilts. On each end, fold over ½" and then fold ½" again. Press and stitch by machine.

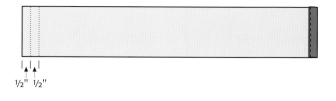

½" ½"

Fold the strip in half lengthwise, wrong sides together; baste the raw edges to the top edge of the back of your quilt. These will be secured when you sew on the binding. Your quilt should be about 1" wider than the sleeve on both sides. Make a little pleat in the sleeve to accommodate the thickness of the rod, and then slipstitch the ends and bottom edge of the sleeve to the backing fabric. This keeps the rod from being inserted next to the quilt backing.

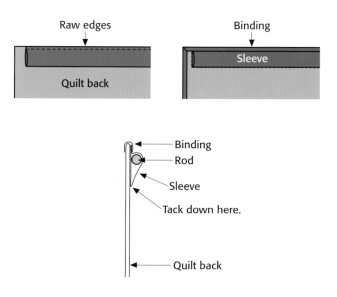

Raw edges

Quilt back

Binding

Sleeve

Binding
Rod
Sleeve
Tack down here.

Quilt back

Adding a Label

FUTURE GENERATIONS WILL want to know more than just who made your quilt and when. Labels can be as elaborate or as simple as you desire. You can write, type, or embroider the information. Be sure to include your name, the name of the quilt, your city and state, the date, the name of the recipient if it is a gift, and any other interesting or important information about the quilt.

Blue Moon
by Nancy Mahoney
Palm Coast, Florida
2001

GARDEN PATH

GARDEN PATH *by Nancy Mahoney. Machine quilted by Lea Wang. The wonderful border fabric has red flowers sprinkled in the cream and green foliage on a black background; it was the color inspiration for this quilt.*

FINISHED QUILT SIZE: 47½" x 59½"
FINISHED BLOCK SIZE: 6" x 6"

MATERIALS

42"-wide fabric

- ¼ yd. total assorted red prints for blocks
- 1 yd. total assorted cream or light yellow prints for blocks
- 1⅜ yds. total assorted black prints for blocks
- ¼ yd. red print for inner border*
- 1½ yds. floral print for outer border
- 2⅞ yds. for backing
- 50" x 62" piece of batting
- ⅜ yd. for binding

* If you prefer to cut the border strips from the lengthwise grain, you will need 1⅜ yards of the red print.

CUTTING

CUT STRIPS ACROSS the width of the fabric unless otherwise indicated.

From the assorted red prints, cut:
- 48 squares, 2¼" x 2¼", for piece 1

From the assorted cream or light yellow prints, cut:
- 14 strips, 2¼" x 42", for pieces 2, 4, and 6

From the assorted black prints, cut:
- 20 strips, 2¼" x 42", for pieces 3, 5, and 7

From the red print for inner border, cut:
- 5 strips, 1½" x 42"

From the floral print for outer border, cut from the lengthwise grain:
- 2 strips, 5" x 52", for sides
- 2 strips, 5" x 49", for top and bottom

From the fabric for binding, cut:
- 6 strips, 2" x 42"

BLOCK CONSTRUCTION

1. Make 48 copies of the Quarter Log Cabin foundation pattern on page 85.

2. Referring to "Blocks Made with Long Strips" on pages 17–18, paper piece 48 Quarter Log Cabin blocks. Start with a red square for piece 1. Use assorted cream or light yellow prints for pieces 2, 4, and 6; use assorted black prints for pieces 3, 5, and 7.

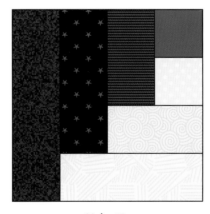

Make 48.

Quilt-Top Assembly

1. Arrange and sew the blocks together in 8 rows of 6 blocks each. Rotate the blocks as needed to form the design. Sew the rows together.

2. Referring to "Borders with Straight-Cut Corners" on pages 21–23, measure and trim the inner-border strips and sew them to the side edges of the quilt top first, and then to the top and bottom edges. Repeat for the outer border.

3. Layer the quilt top with batting and backing; baste. Quilt as desired. Bind the edges and add a sleeve, if desired. Add a label.

PINEAPPLE EXPRESS

PINEAPPLE EXPRESS *by Nancy Mahoney. Machine quilted by Barbara Ford. I used a large variety of red, black, and yellow prints to create this scrappy, sparkling quilt. Any three colors could easily be used in this design.*

FINISHED QUILT SIZE: 58" x 63"
FINISHED BLOCK SIZE: 5" x 5"

MATERIALS

42"-wide fabric

- ⅜ yd. total assorted yellow prints for center square
- 1½ yds. total assorted red prints for blocks
- 1½ yds. total assorted black prints for blocks
- 2⅜ yds. total assorted light prints for blocks
- ¼ yd. yellow print for inner border*
- ¼ yd. red print for middle border*
- 1¾ yds. black print for outer border
- 3⅝ yds. for backing
- 64" x 70" piece of batting
- ½ yd. for binding

* If you prefer to cut the border strips from the lengthwise grain, you will need 1½ yards each of the yellow print and the red print.

CUTTING

CUT STRIPS ACROSS the width of the fabric unless otherwise indicated.

From the assorted yellow prints, cut:
- 90 squares, 2" x 2", for piece 1

From the assorted red prints, cut:
- 90 squares, 2" x 2"; ◻ 180 triangles for pieces 2 and 4
- 90 squares, 2¼" x 2¼"; ◻ 180 triangles for pieces 10 and 12
- 90 squares, 3" x 3"; ◻ 180 triangles for pieces 18 and 20

From the assorted black prints, cut:
- 90 squares, 2" x 2"; ◻ 180 triangles for pieces 3 and 5
- 90 squares, 2¼" x 2¼"; ◻ 180 triangles for pieces 11 and 13
- 90 squares, 3" x 3"; ◻ 180 triangles for pieces 19 and 21

From the assorted light prints, cut:
- 54 strips, 1½" x 42", for pieces 6, 7, 8, 9, 14, 15, 16, and 17

From the yellow print for inner border, cut:
- 5 strips, 1⅜" x 42"

From the red print for middle border, cut:
- 6 strips, 1⅛" x 42"

From the black print for outer border, cut from the lengthwise grain:
- 2 strips, 5¼" x 58", for sides
- 2 strips, 5¼" x 61", for top and bottom

From the fabric for binding, cut:
- 7 strips, 2" x 42"

BLOCK CONSTRUCTION

1. Make 90 copies of the Pineapple foundation pattern on page 86.

2. Referring to "Blocks Made with Cut Pieces" on pages 18–20, paper piece 90 Pineapple blocks. Start with a yellow square for piece 1. Use assorted red prints for pieces 2, 4, 10, 12, 18, and 20; assorted black prints for pieces 3, 5, 11, 13, 19, and 21; and assorted light prints for pieces 6, 7, 8, 9, 14, 15, 16, and 17.

Make 90.

QUILT-TOP ASSEMBLY

1. Arrange and sew the blocks together in 10 rows of 9 blocks each. Sew the rows together.

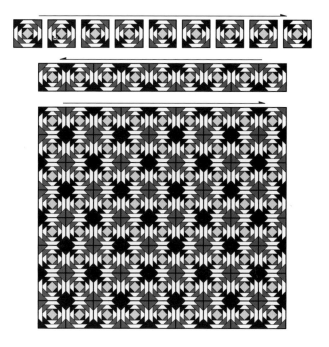

2. Referring to "Borders with Straight-Cut Corners" on pages 21–23, measure and trim the yellow inner-border strips and sew them to the side edges of the quilt top first, and then to the top and bottom edges. Repeat for the red middle border and black outer border.

3. Layer the quilt top with batting and backing; baste. Quilt as desired. Bind the edges and add a sleeve, if desired. Add a label.

T-TIME

T-TIME *by Nancy Mahoney. Machine quilted by Lea Wang. The nontraditional setting of the T blocks creates an unexpected secondary pattern. The variety of background prints adds dimension to the quilt.*

FINISHED QUILT SIZE: 41" x 45"
FINISHED BLOCK SIZE: 4" x 4"

MATERIALS

42"-wide fabric

- 1 yd. assorted medium to dark prints for blocks

- 1¼ yds. assorted light prints for blocks
- ⅜ yd. red print for inner border
- ¾ yd. black print for outer border
- 1½ yds. for backing
- 47" x 51" piece of batting
- ⅜ yd. for binding

CUTTING

CUT STRIPS ACROSS the width of the fabric unless otherwise indicated.

From the assorted medium to dark prints, cut:
- 56 rectangles, 2½" x 3½", for piece 1
- 56 squares, 2¾" x 2¾"; ◻ 112 triangles for pieces 4 and 5 (2 for each block to match a piece 1 rectangle)

From the assorted light prints, cut:
- 140 squares, 2¼" x 2¼"; ◻ 280 triangles for pieces 2, 3, 7, 8, and 9
- 28 squares, 4" x 4"; ◻ 56 triangles for piece 6

From the red print for inner border, cut:
- 4 strips, 2" x 42"

From the black print for outer border, cut:
- 4 strips, 5¼" x 42"

From the fabric for binding, cut:
- 5 strips, 2" x 42"

BLOCK CONSTRUCTION

1. Make 56 copies of the T Block foundation pattern on page 87.

2. Referring to "Blocks Made with Cut Pieces" on pages 18–20, paper piece 56 T blocks. Start with a medium or dark rectangle for piece 1. Use the same medium or dark print for pieces 4 and 5. Use a light print for pieces 2, 3, 6, 7, 8, and 9.

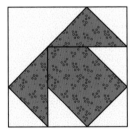

Make 56.

QUILT-TOP ASSEMBLY

1. Arrange and sew the blocks together in 8 rows of 7 blocks each, alternating the direction of the blocks across the rows. Sew the rows together.

2. Sew 1 red border strip to 1 black border strip. Repeat for the other 3 strips. The inner and outer borders are now used as 1 border.

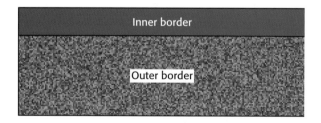

3. Referring to "Borders with Straight-Cut Corners" on pages 21–23, measure and trim the border strips and sew them to the side edges of the quilt top first, and then to the top and bottom edges.

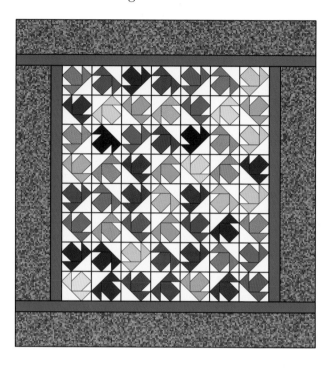

4. Layer the quilt top with batting and backing; baste. Quilt as desired. Bind the edges and add a sleeve, if desired. Add a label.

SPOOLIN' AROUND

SPOOLIN' AROUND *by Nancy Mahoney. Machine quilted by Gretchen Engle. The Spool block is one of my favorite blocks. A different fabric is used in each block to create a very scrappy look.*

FINISHED QUILT SIZE: 31½" x 37½"
FINISHED BLOCK SIZE: 3" x 3"

MATERIALS

42"-wide fabric

- 1 yd. total assorted light prints for blocks
- 1¼ yds. total assorted multicolored prints for blocks
- ¼ yd. purple print for inner border
- ⅜ yd. multicolored print for outer border
- 1 yd. for backing
- 38" x 44" piece of batting
- ⅜ yd. for binding

CUTTING

CUT STRIPS ACROSS the width of the fabric unless otherwise indicated.

From the assorted light prints, cut:
- 160 rectangles, 1½" x 4", for piece 1 of units A and B

From the assorted multicolored prints, cut:
- 160 squares, 2¼" x 2¼"; ◻ 320 triangles for pieces 2 and 3 of units A and B
- 80 rectangles, 2" x 4", for piece 4 of unit A

From the purple print for inner border, cut:
- 4 strips, 1½" x 42"

From the multicolored print for outer border, cut:
- 4 strips, 3" x 42"

From the fabric for binding, cut:
- 4 strips, 2" x 42"

BLOCK CONSTRUCTION

1. Make 80 copies of the Spools foundation pattern on page 88.

2. Referring to "Blocks Made with Cut Pieces" on pages 18–20, paper piece 80 Spools blocks. Start with a light rectangle for piece 1 of both unit A and B. Use the same multicolored print for pieces 2, 3, and 4 of unit A and for pieces 2 and 3 of unit B.

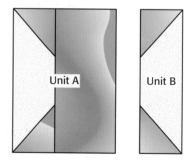

Make 80 each.

3. Remove the paper foundation from each unit and sew unit A to unit B to complete the block.

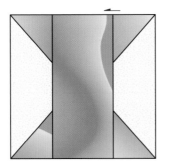

Sew unit A to unit B.

QUILT-TOP ASSEMBLY

1. Arrange and sew the blocks together in 10 rows of 8 blocks each, alternating the direction of the spools across the rows. Sew the rows together.

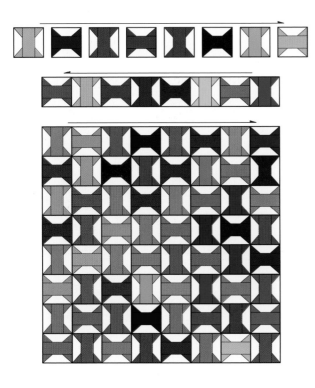

2. Referring to "Borders with Straight-Cut Corners" on pages 21–23, measure and trim the inner-border strips and sew them to the side edges of the quilt top first, and then to the top and bottom edges. Repeat for the outer border.

3. Layer the quilt top with batting and backing; baste. Quilt as desired. Bind the edges and add a sleeve, if desired. Add a label.

Confetti

Confetti *by Nancy Mahoney. Machine quilted by Barbara Ford. My passion for batik fabrics has resulted in an extensive stash, which I used in designing this quilt. The important component is the contrast between the very light and very dark fabrics to create movement and hidden stars.*

FINISHED QUILT SIZE: 52¾" x 62¾"
FINISHED BLOCK SIZE: 5" x 5"

MATERIALS

42"-wide fabric

- 2¾ yds. total assorted light batiks for blocks
- 2¾ yds. total assorted dark batiks for blocks

- ¼ yd. yellow batik for inner border*
- 1⅝ yds. multicolor batik for outer border
- 3⅜ yds. for backing
- 60" x 70" piece of batting
- ½ yd. for binding

* If you prefer to cut the border strips from the lengthwise grain, you will need 1⅝ yards of the yellow batik.

CUTTING

CUT STRIPS ACROSS the width of the fabric unless otherwise indicated.

From the assorted light batiks, cut:
- 50 squares, 2¼" x 2¼", for piece 1 of block B
- 98 squares, 2" x 2"; ◻ 196 triangles for pieces 2, 3, 4, and 5 of block A
- 100 squares, 2½" x 2½"; ◻ 200 triangles for pieces 6, 7, 8, and 9 of block B
- 98 squares, 3¼" x 3¼"; ◻ 196 triangles for pieces 10, 11, 12, and 13 of block A

From the assorted dark batiks, cut:
- 49 squares, 2¼" x 2¼", for piece 1 of block A
- 100 squares, 2" x 2"; ◻ 200 triangles for pieces 2, 3, 4, and 5 of block B
- 98 squares, 2½" x 2½"; ◻ 196 triangles for pieces 6, 7, 8, and 9 of block A
- 100 squares, 3¼" x 3¼"; ◻ 200 triangles for pieces 10, 11, 12, and 13 of block B

From the yellow batik for inner border, cut:
- 5 strips, 1⅛" x 42"

From the multicolor batik for outer border, cut from the lengthwise grain:
- 2 strips, 3½" x 58", for sides
- 2 strips, 3½" x 54", for top and bottom

From the fabric for binding, cut:
- 7 strips, 2" x 42"

BLOCK CONSTRUCTION

1. Make 99 copies of the Square-on-Square foundation pattern on page 89.

2. Referring to "Blocks Made with Cut Pieces" on pages 18–20, paper piece 49 Square-on-Square blocks for block A. Start with a dark square for piece 1. Use light batiks for pieces 2, 3, 4, 5, 10, 11, 12, and 13; and dark batiks for pieces 6, 7, 8, and 9.

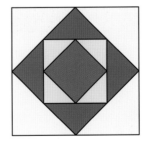

Block A
Make 49.

3. Paper piece 50 Square-on-Square blocks for block B, starting with a light square for piece 1. Use dark batiks for pieces 2, 3, 4, 5, 10, 11, 12, and 13; and light batiks for pieces 6, 7, 8, and 9.

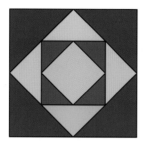

Block B
Make 50.

QUILT-TOP ASSEMBLY

1. Arrange and sew the blocks into 11 rows of 9 blocks each, alternating blocks A and B in each row. Sew the rows together.

2. Referring to "Borders with Straight-Cut Corners" on pages 21–23, measure and trim the inner-border strips and sew them to the side edges of the quilt top first, and then to the top and bottom edges. Repeat for the outer border.

3. Layer the quilt top with batting and backing; baste. Quilt as desired. Bind the edges and add a sleeve, if desired. Add a label.

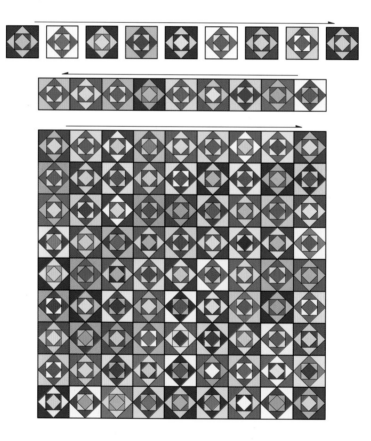

CINNAMON AND SPICE

CINNAMON AND SPICE *by Nancy Mahoney. Machine quilted by Gretchen Engle. The easy pieced border repeats the triangles that surround the stars. The dark stars sparkle against the light background.*

FINISHED QUILT SIZE: 38½" x 44½"
FINISHED BLOCK SIZE: 3" x 3"

MATERIALS

42"-wide fabric

- 1 yd. total assorted light prints for Four-Patch Star blocks and border blocks
- ¾ yd. total assorted rust, brown, and black prints for Four-Patch Star blocks
- ¼ yd. rust print for border and corner blocks
- 1 yd. dark brown print for border and corner blocks and outer border
- ¼ yd. light print for inner border
- 1⅜ yds. for backing
- 45" x 51" piece of batting
- ⅜ yd. for binding

CUTTING

CUT STRIPS ACROSS the width of the fabric unless otherwise indicated.

From the assorted light prints, cut:
- 80 rectangles, 2¼" x 4", for piece 1 of Four-Patch Star block
- 40 squares, 2¾" x 2¾"; △ 80 triangles for piece 4 of Four-Patch Star block
- 15 squares, 3½" x 3½"; ⊠ 60 triangles for piece 1 of border blocks; you will have 2 triangles left over

From the assorted rust, brown, and black prints, cut:
- 40 squares, 2¾" x 2¾"; △ 80 triangles for piece 2 of Four-Patch Star block
- 80 rectangles, 2¼" x 4", for piece 3 of Four-Patch Star block

From the rust print, cut:
- 16 squares, 3½" x 3½"; ⊠ 64 triangles for piece 2 of border and corner blocks; you will have 2 triangles left over

From the dark brown print, cut:
- 31 squares, 3¼" x 3¼"; △ 62 triangles for piece 3 of border and corner blocks
- 1 square, 3½" x 3½"; ⊠ 4 triangles for piece 1 of corner blocks
- 4 strips, 4¼" x 42", for outer border

From the light print for inner border, cut:
- 4 strips, 1¾" x 42"

From the fabric for binding, cut:
- 5 strips, 2" x 42"

BLOCK CONSTRUCTION

1. Make 80 copies of the Four-Patch Star foundation pattern on page 90.

2. Referring to "Blocks Made with Cut Pieces" on pages 18–20, paper piece 80 Four-Patch Star blocks. Start with a light print for piece 1. Use assorted rust, brown, and black prints for pieces 2 and 3 and a light print for piece 4. Make 20 sets of 4 blocks that use the same fabric for piece 3.

Four-Patch Star Block
Make 20 sets of 4 blocks
that use the same fabric for piece 3.

3. Make 62 copies of the border foundation pattern on page 90.

4. Paper piece 58 border blocks, starting with a light print for piece 1. Use a rust print for piece 2 and a dark brown print for piece 3.

Border Block
Make 58.

5. Paper piece 4 border blocks for the corners. Use a dark brown print for pieces 1 and 3. Use a rust print for piece 2.

Corner Block
Make 4.

QUILT-TOP ASSEMBLY

1. Arrange and sew together 4 Four-Patch Star blocks with matching piece 3 to make 1 large block.

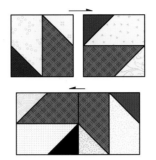 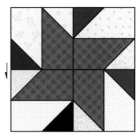

Make 20.

2. Arrange and sew the larger blocks into 5 rows of 4 blocks each. Rotate the blocks so the middle horizontal seams butt. Sew the rows together.

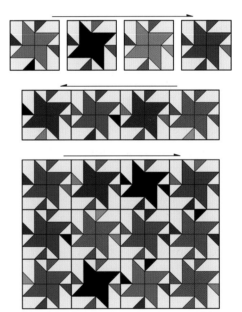

3. Referring to "Borders with Straight-Cut Corners" on pages 21–23, measure and trim the light inner-border strips and sew them to the side edges of the quilt top first, and then to the top and bottom edges.

   NOTE: *After you add the inner border, the quilt top must measure 26½" x 32½" (including seam allowances) for the pieced border to fit properly. Adjust the width of the inner border if necessary to achieve the correct size.*

4. Sew 16 border blocks together to make each of the side border strips. Sew 13 border blocks together to make each of the top and bottom border strips, adding a corner block to each end.

Side Borders
Make 2.

Top and Bottom Borders
Make 2.

5. Sew the side border strips to opposite sides of the quilt top, placing the light triangles toward the inner border. Add the top and bottom border strips, again placing the light triangles toward the inner border.

6. Measure, trim, and sew outer-border strips as for inner border.

7. Layer the quilt top with batting and backing; baste. Quilt as desired. Bind the edges and add a sleeve, if desired. Add a label.

BLUE MOON

BLUE MOON *by Nancy Mahoney. Machine quilted by Lea Wang.*
This quilt showcases an all-time favorite color combination.
The blue fabrics create the look of a traditional quilt; use novelty
fabrics for a fun child's quilt.

FINISHED QUILT SIZE: 44½" x 56½"
FINISHED BLOCK SIZE: 6" x 6"

MATERIALS

42"-wide fabric

- 1⅝ yds. total assorted blue prints for blocks
- 1¼ yds total assorted light prints for blocks
- 1⅜ yds. blue print for border
- 2⅞ yds. for backing
- 50" x 62" piece of batting
- ⅜ yd. for binding

CUTTING

CUT STRIPS ACROSS the width of the fabric unless otherwise indicated.

From the assorted blue prints, cut:
- 48 squares, 2¼" x 2¼", for piece 1
- 24 squares, 4" x 4"; ◺ 48 triangles for piece 4
- 24 squares, 7½" x 7½"; ◺ 48 triangles for piece 7

From the assorted light prints, cut:
- 48 squares, 2¾" x 2¾"; ◺ 96 triangles for pieces 2 and 3
- 48 squares, 4" x 4"; ◺ 96 triangles for pieces 5 and 6

From the blue print for border, cut from the lengthwise grain:
- 2 strips, 4½" x 50", for sides
- 2 strips, 4½" x 47", for top and bottom

From the fabric for binding, cut:
- 5 strips, 2" x 42"

BLOCK CONSTRUCTION

1. Make 48 copies of the Arrowhead foundation pattern on page 91.

2. Referring to "Blocks Made with Cut Pieces" on pages 18–20, paper piece 48 Arrowhead blocks. Start with a blue print for piece 1. Use assorted light prints for pieces 2, 3, 5, and 6; use assorted blue prints for pieces 4 and 7.

Make 48.

QUILT-TOP ASSEMBLY

1. Arrange and sew the blocks together in 8 rows of 6 blocks each. Rotate the blocks as needed to form the design. Sew the rows together.

2. Referring to "Borders with Straight-Cut Corners" on pages 21–23, measure and trim the border strips and sew them to the side edges of the quilt top first, and then to the top and bottom edges.

3. Layer the quilt top with batting and backing; baste. Quilt as desired. Bind the edges and add a sleeve, if desired. Add a label.

OPTICAL FIBERS

OPTICAL FIBERS *by Nancy Mahoney. Machine quilted by Lea Wang. The use of an accent fabric in the last row of blocks, combined with darker fabrics in the outer positions, gives the illusion of a pieced inner border.*

FINISHED QUILT SIZE: 37½" x 49½"
FINISHED BLOCK SIZE: 6" x 6"

MATERIALS

42"-wide fabric

- 1¾ yds. total assorted purple prints for blocks
- 1 yd. total assorted yellow prints for blocks
- ⅝ yd. yellow-and-green floral print for border and corner blocks
- 1⅜ yds. purple print for border
- 1½ yds. for backing
- 43" x 55" piece of batting
- ⅜ yd. for binding

CUTTING

CUT STRIPS ACROSS the width of the fabric unless otherwise indicated.

From the assorted purple prints, cut:
- 13 strips, 3½" x 42", for blocks
- 46 squares, 3" x 3"; ◻ 92 triangles for blocks

From the assorted yellow prints, cut:
- 6 strips, 3½" x 42", for blocks
- 24 squares, 3" x 3"; ◻ 48 triangles for blocks

From the yellow-and-green floral print, cut:
- 5 strips, 3½" x 42", for border and corner blocks

From the purple print for border, cut from the lengthwise grain:
- 2 strips, 4" x 44", for sides
- 2 strips, 4" x 39", for top and bottom

From the fabric for binding, cut:
- 5 strips, 2" x 42"

BLOCK CONSTRUCTION

1. Make 35 copies of the Kaleidoscope foundation pattern on page 92.

2. Referring to "Blocks Made with Long Strips" and "Blocks Made with Cut Pieces" on pages 17–20, paper piece 7 Kaleidoscope blocks with yellow corners. For units A and B, use purple prints for pieces 1 and 3; use yellow prints for pieces 2, 4, 5, and 6. Remove the paper foundation from each unit and sew unit A to unit B to complete the block.

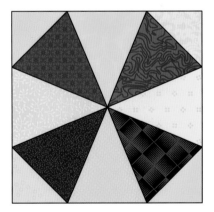

Block with Yellow Corners
Make 7.

3. Paper piece 8 Kaleidoscope blocks with purple corners. For units A and B, use yellow prints for pieces 1 and 3; use purple prints for pieces 2, 4, 5, and 6. Remove the paper foundation from each unit and sew unit A to unit B.

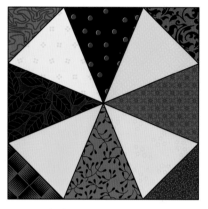

Block with Purple Corners
Make 8.

4. Paper piece 10 Kaleidoscope border blocks with 2 yellow corners. For unit A, use purple prints for pieces 1, 3, and 5. Use yellow prints for pieces 4 and 6; use the yellow-and-green floral print for piece 2. For unit B, use purple prints for pieces 1, 3, 4, and 5. Use a yellow print for piece 6; use a yellow-and-green floral for piece 2. Remove the paper foundation from each unit and sew unit A to unit B.

Border Block with 2 Yellow Corners
Make 10.

5. Paper piece 6 Kaleidoscope border blocks with purple corners. For unit A, use purple prints for pieces 1, 4, 5, and 6. Use a yellow print for piece 3; use a yellow-and-green floral for piece 2. For unit B, use purple prints for pieces 3, 4, 5, and 6. Use a yellow print for piece 1, and a yellow-and-green print for piece 2. Remove the paper foundation from each unit and sew unit A to unit B.

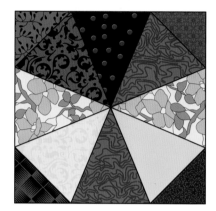

Border Block with Purple Corners
Make 6.

6. Paper piece 4 Kaleidoscope corner blocks. For unit A, use purple prints for pieces 1, 2, 3, 5, and 6. Use a yellow-and-green floral for piece 4. For unit B, use a yellow print in piece 1 and a yellow-and-green floral for piece 2. Use purple prints for pieces 3, 4, 5, and 6. Remove the paper foundation from each unit and sew unit A to unit B.

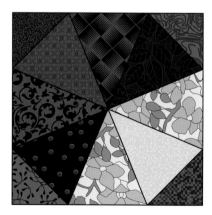

Corner Block
Make 4.

QUILT-TOP ASSEMBLY

1. Arrange the blocks in 7 rows of 5 blocks each, paying careful attention to the placement. Sew the blocks together in rows. Join the rows.

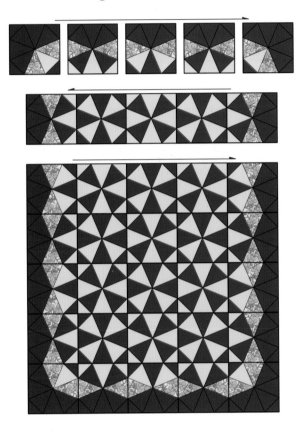

2. Referring to "Borders with Straight-Cut Corners" on pages 21–23, measure and trim the border strips and sew them to the side edges of the quilt top first, and then to the top and bottom edges.

3. Layer the quilt top with batting and backing; baste. Quilt as desired. Bind the edges and add a sleeve, if desired. Add a label.

CROSSING THE BLUES

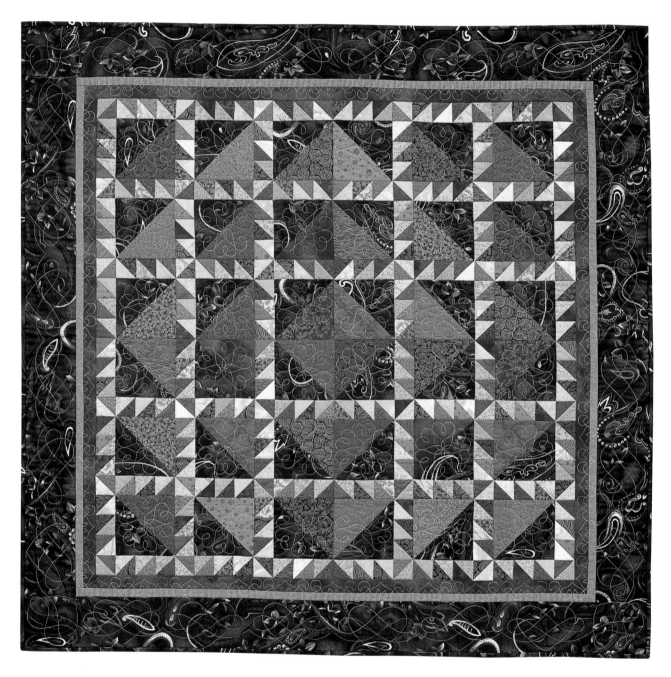

CROSSING THE BLUES *by Nancy Mahoney. Machine quilted by Lea Wang. The colors in this quilt remind me of the clear blue skies and green forests you see as you cross the Blue Mountains in eastern Oregon. This design would be just as exciting in a different color combination.*

Finished quilt size: 47¾" x 47¾"
Finished block size: 6" x 6"

Materials

42"-wide fabric

- 1¼ yds. total assorted blue prints for blocks
- ¾ yd. total assorted gold prints for blocks
- 1½ yds. green print for blocks and outer border
- ¼ yd. blue print for inner border
- ¼ yd. gold print for middle border
- 3 yds. for backing
- 52" x 52" piece of batting
- ⅜ yd. for binding

Cutting

Cut strips across the width of the fabric unless otherwise indicated.

From the assorted blue prints, cut:
- 126 squares, 2½" x 2½"; ◻ 252 triangles for pieces 1, 3, 5, and 7 of unit A and pieces 1, 3, and 5 of unit B
- 18 squares, 5¾" x 5¾"; ◻ 36 triangles for piece 8 of unit B

From the assorted gold prints, cut:
- 126 squares, 2½" x 2½"; ◻ 252 triangles for pieces 2, 4, 6, and 8 of unit A and pieces 2, 4, and 6 of unit B

From the green print, cut from the lengthwise grain:
- 2 strips, 4½" x 42", for side outer-border strips
- 2 strips, 4½" x 50", for top and bottom outer-border strips
- 18 squares, 5¾" x 5¾"; ◻ 36 triangles for piece 7 of unit B

From the blue print for inner border, cut:
- 2 strips, 1½" x 38", for sides
- 2 strips, 1½" x 40", for top and bottom

From the gold print for middle border, cut:
- 2 strips, 1⅛" x 40", for sides
- 2 strips, 1⅛" x 42", for top and bottom

From the fabric for binding, cut:
- 5 strips, 2" x 42"

BLOCK CONSTRUCTION

1. Make 36 copies of the Delectable Mountain foundation pattern on page 93.

2. Referring to "Blocks Made with Cut Pieces" on pages 18–20, paper piece 36 Delectable Mountain blocks. For unit A, use gold prints for pieces 2, 4, 6, and 8; use blue prints for pieces 1, 3, 5, and 7. For unit B, use gold prints for pieces 2, 4, and 6; use blue prints for pieces 1, 3, 5, and 8; use a green print for piece 7.

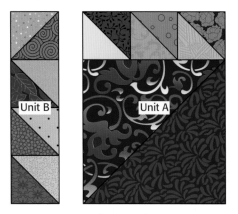

Make 36 each.

3. Remove the paper foundation from each unit and sew unit A to unit B.

Sew unit A to unit B.

QUILT-TOP ASSEMBLY

1. Arrange and sew the blocks together in 6 rows of 6 blocks each. Rotate the blocks as needed to form the design. Sew the rows together.

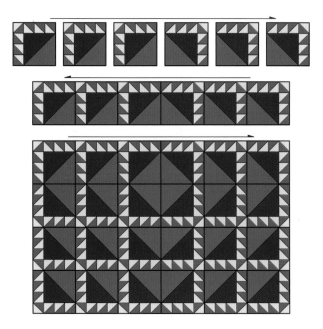

2. Referring to "Borders with Straight-Cut Corners" on pages 21–23, measure and trim the inner-border strips and sew them to the side edges of the quilt top first, and then to the top and bottom edges. Repeat for the middle and outer borders.

3. Layer the quilt top with batting and backing; baste. Quilt as desired. Bind the edges and add a sleeve, if desired. Add a label.

TWIST AND SHOUT

TWIST AND SHOUT *by Nancy Mahoney. Machine quilted by Lea Wang. The jewel-tone blocks appear to float on the black batik background. A light background with dark blocks would also be very effective.*

Finished quilt size: 48½" x 48½"
Finished block size: 6" x 6"

Materials

42"-wide fabric

- 1½ yds. total assorted bright batiks in several color families for blocks

- 1¾ yds. black batik for blocks and inner border
- 1½ yds. blue batik for outer border
- 3 yds. for backing
- 52" x 52" piece of batting
- ⅜ yd. for binding

Cutting

CUT STRIPS ACROSS the width of the fabric unless otherwise indicated.

From the assorted bright batiks, cut:
- 36 squares, 2" x 2", for piece 1
- 36 squares, 1¾" x 1¾"; ◻ 72 triangles for pieces 2 and 4
- 36 squares, 2¼" x 2¼"; ◻ 72 triangles for pieces 7 and 9
- 36 squares, 3" x 3"; ◻ 72 triangles for pieces 10 and 12
- 36 squares, 4¼" x 4¼"; ◻ 72 triangles for pieces 15 and 17

From the black batik, cut:
- 36 squares, 1¾" x 1¾"; ◻ 72 triangles for pieces 3 and 5
- 36 squares, 2¼" x 2¼"; ◻ 72 triangles for pieces 6 and 8

- 36 squares, 3" x 3"; ◻ 72 triangles for pieces 11 and 13
- 36 squares, 4¼" x 4¼"; ◻ 72 triangles for pieces 14 and 16
- 2 strips, 2½" x 38", for side inner-border strips
- 2 strips, 2½" x 42", for top and bottom inner-border strips

From the blue batik for outer border, cut from the lengthwise grain:
- 2 strips, 4½" x 42", for sides
- 2 strips, 4½" x 50", for top and bottom

From the fabric for binding, cut:
- 5 strips, 2" x 42"

Block Construction

1. Make 36 copies of the Virginia Reel foundation pattern on page 94.

2. Referring to "Blocks Made with Cut Pieces" on pages 18–20, paper piece 36 Virginia Reel blocks. Use assorted bright batiks in one color family for pieces 1, 2, 7, 12, and 17. Use

assorted bright batiks in a second color family for pieces 4, 9, 10, and 15. Use black batik for pieces 3, 5, 6, 8, 11, 13, 14, and 16.

Make 36.

QUILT-TOP ASSEMBLY

1. Arrange and sew the blocks together in 6 rows of 6 blocks each. Sew the rows together.

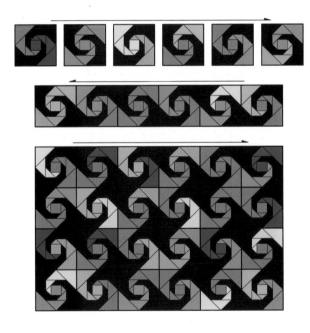

2. Referring to "Borders with Straight-Cut Corners" on pages 21–23, measure and trim the inner-border strips and sew them to the side edges of the quilt top first, and then to the top and bottom edges. Repeat for the outer border.

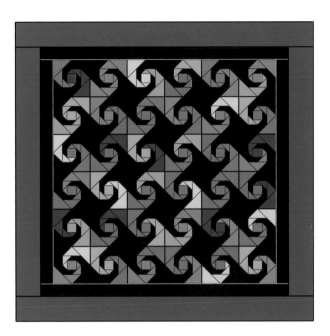

3. Layer the quilt top with batting and backing; baste. Quilt as desired. Bind the edges and add a sleeve, if desired. Add a label.

SWIMMING UPSTREAM

SWIMMING UPSTREAM *by Nancy Mahoney. Machine quilted by Gretchen Engle. The fish print and Ocean Waves block are a natural combination for a quilter in the Pacific Northwest. This design could easily work with a different theme fabric.*

MATERIALS

42"-wide fabric

- 1¾ yds. total assorted gold prints for blocks
- 1¼ yds. total assorted navy prints for blocks
- 1½ yds. fish print for blocks and border
- 3 yds. for backing
- 52" x 64" piece of batting
- ⅜ yd. for binding

CUTTING

CUT STRIPS ACROSS the width of the fabric unless otherwise indicated.

From the assorted gold prints, cut:

- 120 squares, 3¼" x 3¼"; ◻ 240 triangles for pieces 1, 3, and 5 of unit A and pieces 2 and 4 of unit B
- 24 squares, each 5¼" x 5¼"; ◻ 48 triangles for piece 6 of unit A

From the assorted navy prints, cut:

- 120 squares, 3¼" x 3¼"; ◻ 240 triangles for pieces 2 and 4 of unit A and pieces 1, 3, and 5 of unit B

From the fish print, cut from the lengthwise grain (cut borders first):

- 2 strips, 5½" x 50", for side border strips
- 2 strips, 5½" x 48", for top and bottom border strips
- 24 squares, 5¼" x 5¼"; ◻ 48 triangles for piece 6 of unit B

From the fabric for binding, cut:

- 6 strips, 2" x 42"

BLOCK CONSTRUCTION

1. Make 48 copies of the Ocean Waves foundation pattern on page 95.

2. Referring to "Blocks Made with Cut Pieces" on pages 18–20, paper piece 48 Ocean Waves blocks. For unit A, use gold prints for pieces 1, 3, 5, and 6, and navy prints for pieces 2 and 4. For unit B, use navy prints for pieces 1, 3, and 5; gold prints for pieces 2 and 4; and a fish print for piece 6.

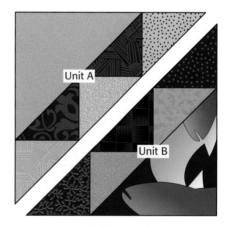

Make 48 each.

3. Remove the paper foundation from each unit and sew unit A to unit B to complete the block.

Sew unit A to unit B.

QUILT-TOP ASSEMBLY

1. Arrange and sew the blocks together in 8 rows of 6 blocks each. Rotate blocks as needed to form the design. Sew the rows together.

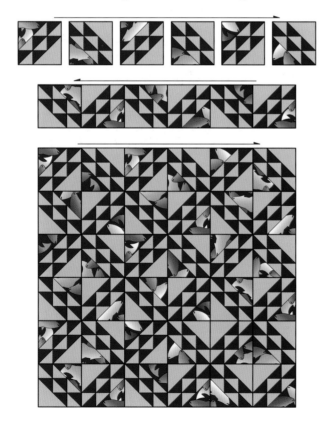

2. Referring to "Borders with Straight-Cut Corners" on pages 21–23, measure and trim the border strips and sew them to the side edges of the quilt top first, and then to the top and bottom edges.

3. Layer the quilt top with batting and backing; baste. Quilt as desired. Bind the edges and add a sleeve, if desired. Add a label.

Autumn Leaves

AUTUMN LEAVES *by Nancy Mahoney. Machine quilted by Sue Lohse. The setting and different block sizes make the leaves appear to be swirling around in the wind.*

FINISHED QUILT SIZE: 31½" x 37½"
FINISHED BLOCK SIZES: 5" x 5", 6" x 6",
7" x 7"

MATERIALS

42"-wide fabric

- 1 yd. total assorted prints for leaves
- 1⅛ yds. total assorted black prints for blocks and sashing
- ⅛ yd. total assorted prints for stems
- ½ yd. black print for border
- 1¼ yds. for backing
- 37" x 43" piece of batting
- ⅜ yd. for binding

CUTTING

CUT STRIPS ACROSS the width of the fabric unless otherwise indicated.

From the assorted prints for leaves, cut:
- 12 strips, 2½" x 42", for pieces 2, 3, 4, and 6 of units A and B

From the assorted black prints, cut:
- 3 strips, 2" x 42", for piece 1 of 5", 6", and 7" blocks
- 1 strip, 2¼" x 42", for piece 7 of 5" blocks
- 1 strip, 2½" x 42", for piece 7 of 6" blocks
- 1 strip, 2¾" x 42", for piece 5 of 5" blocks
- 1 strip, 3" x 42", for piece 7 of 7" blocks
- 2 strips, 3½" x 42", for piece 5 of 6" and 7" blocks

From the assorted prints for stems, cut:
- 12 strips, ¾" x 9"

From the black print for border, cut:
- 4 strips, 3½" x 42"

From the fabric for binding, cut:
- 4 strips, 2" x 42"

BLOCK CONSTRUCTION

1. Make copies of the Autumn Leaf foundation patterns on pages 96–99. Make 3 copies of the 5" pattern, 5 copies of the 6" pattern, and 4 copies of the 7" pattern.

2. Referring to "Blocks Made with Long Strips" and "Blocks Made with Cut Pieces" on pages 17–20, paper piece the Autumn Leaf blocks. For unit A and unit B, use a black print for piece 1; leaf-colored prints for pieces 2, 3, 4, and 6; and black prints for pieces 5 and 7. Make the A and B units for all the blocks, but do not sew the units together yet. Remove the paper foundation from each unit.

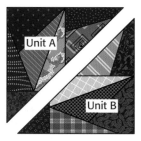

Make 3 each for 5" block,
5 each for 6" block,
and 4 each for 7" block.

3. Fold a ¾" x 9" strip for the stem in half with the wrong sides together and press. Place the raw edges of the folded strip along the diagonal edge of unit A so that the end of the stem stops about 1" from the tip of the leaf. Shift the stem slightly so the end runs off the edge at an angle. Starting with a ⅛"-wide seam, sew from the bottom of the leaf to the top, angling the stitching so the seam runs off the folded edge of the stem near the top. The stem should fade out of the seam before the leaf point. Sew unit A to unit B with a ¼"-wide seam to complete the block. Repeat for all blocks.

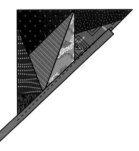 

Sew unit A to unit B.

QUILT-TOP ASSEMBLY

1. Cut sashing strips from the assorted black prints as indicated.

Sashing Position	Cutting Dimensions	No. of Pieces
A	1½" x 5½"	2
B	1½" x 6½"	3
C	1½" x 7½"	1
D	1½" x 14"	1
E	2" x 6½"	1
F	2" x 7½"	7
G	2¼" x 7½"	4
H	2½" x 5½"	2
I	2½" x 31½"	2

2. Arrange and sew the blocks and sashing strips together.

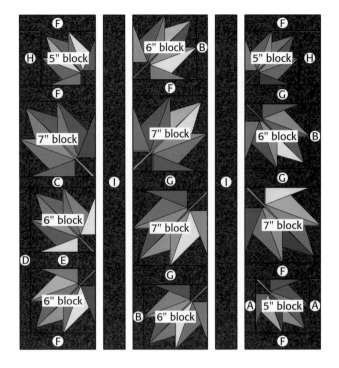

3. Referring to "Borders with Straight-Cut Corners" on pages 21–23, measure and trim the border strips and sew them to the side edges of the quilt top first, and then to the top and bottom edges.

4. Layer the quilt top with batting and backing; baste. Quilt as desired. Bind the edges and add a sleeve, if desired. Add a label.

PINEAPPLE SPLASH

PINEAPPLE SPLASH *by Nancy Mahoney. Machine quilted by Barbara Ford. The side-by-side setting of the Off-Center Pineapple block creates a wonderful design of circles and a feeling of motion.*

FINISHED QUILT SIZE: 48½" x 60½"
FINISHED BLOCK SIZE: 6" x 6"

MATERIALS

42"-wide fabric

- 2 yds. total assorted light prints for blocks
- 2½ yds. total assorted medium and dark prints for blocks
- ¼ yd. dark print for inner border*

- ⅜ yd. yellow print for middle border*
- 1⅝ yds. dark print for outer border
- 3 yds. for backing
- 54" x 66" piece of batting
- ⅜ yd. for binding

* If you prefer to cut the borders from the lengthwise grain, you will need 1½ yards each of the dark print and the yellow print.

CUTTING

CUT STRIPS ACROSS the width of the fabric unless otherwise indicated.

From the assorted light prints, cut:
- 23 strips, 1⅝" x 42", for pieces 2, 5, 10, 11, 19, and 20
- 24 strips, 1⅛" x 42", for pieces 3, 4, 12, 13, 18, and 21

From the assorted medium and dark prints, cut:
- 48 squares, 2" x 2", for piece 1
- 16 strips, 1⅝" x 42", for pieces 6, 15, and 22
- 10 strips, 1" x 42", for pieces 8, 17, and 26
- 24 squares, 2¾" x 2¾"; ◻ 48 triangles for piece 23
- 24 squares, 2" x 2"; ◻ 48 triangles for piece 27
- 144 rectangles, 2" x 4"; cut 72 rectangles once diagonally from top left to bottom right

as shown to yield half rectangles; cut 72 rectangles once diagonally from bottom left to top right as shown to yield reverse half rectangles.

Cut 72 rectangles to yield 144 half rectangles for pieces 7, 16, and 24.

Cut 72 rectangles to yield 144 reverse half rectangles for pieces 9, 14, and 25.

From the dark print for inner border, cut:
- 5 strips, 1½" x 42"

From the yellow print for middle border, cut:
- 5 strips, 2" x 42"

From the dark print for outer border, cut from the lengthwise grain:
- 2 strips, 4" x 55", for sides
- 2 strips, 4" x 51", for top and bottom

From the fabric for binding, cut:
- 6 strips, 2" x 42"

BLOCK CONSTRUCTION

1. Make 48 copies of the Off-Center Pineapple foundation pattern on page 100.

2. Referring to "Blocks Made with Long Strips" and "Blocks Made with Cut Pieces" on pages 17–20, paper piece 48 Off-Center Pineapple blocks. Start with a medium or dark print for piece 1. Use 1⅝"-wide light strips for pieces 2, 5, 10, 11, 19, and 20; and the 1⅛"-wide light strips for pieces 3, 4, 12, 13, 18, and 21. Use 1⅝"-wide medium and dark strips for pieces 6, 15, and 22; and 1"-wide medium and dark strips for pieces 8, 17, and 26. Use a 2¾" half-square triangle for piece 23, and a 2" half-square triangle for piece 27. Use half-rectangle triangles for pieces 7, 16, and 24; and reversed half-rectangle triangles for pieces 9, 14, and 25.

Make 48.

QUILT-TOP ASSEMBLY

1. Arrange and sew the blocks together in 8 rows of 6 blocks each. Rotate blocks as needed to form the design. Sew the rows together.

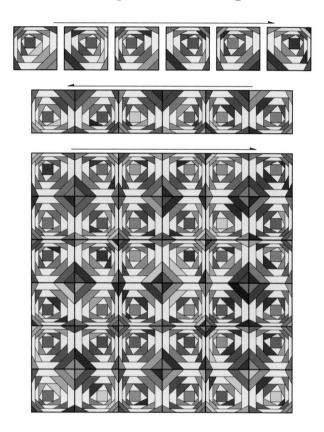

2. Referring to "Borders with Straight-Cut Corners" on pages 21–23, measure and trim the inner-border strips and sew them to the side edges of the quilt top first, and then to the top and bottom edges. Repeat for the middle border and outer border.

3. Layer the quilt top with batting and backing; baste. Quilt as desired. Bind the edges and add a sleeve, if desired. Add a label.

RED CHILI PEPPERS

RED CHILI PEPPERS *by Nancy Mahoney. Machine quilted by Lea Wang. The red and black fabrics create a dramatic and sophisticated quilt. For a more a traditional look, use a light fabric for the background.*

FINISHED QUILT SIZE: 50⅝" x 50⅝"
FINISHED BLOCK SIZE: 8" x 8"

MATERIALS

42"-wide fabric

- 1¼ yds. total assorted red prints for blocks
- ⅝ yd. total assorted black tone-on-tone prints for blocks
- 1⅜ yds. total assorted black-and-red prints for blocks and sashing

- 1½ yds. black-and-red print for inner and outer borders
- ¼ yd. red print for middle border*
- 3⅛ yds. for backing
- 56" x 56" piece of batting
- ⅜ yd. for binding

* If you prefer to cut the border strips from the length-wise grain, you will need 1¼ yards of the red print.

CUTTING

CUT STRIPS ACROSS the width of the fabric unless otherwise indicated.

From the assorted red prints, cut:
- 9 strips, 2" x 42", for pieces 2, 4, 6, 8, 10, 12, and 14
- 41 squares, 1⅞" x 1⅞", for blocks and sashing squares
- 16 of piece B (page 102) for block centers

From the assorted black tone-on-tone prints, cut:
- 10 strips, 2" x 42", for pieces 1, 3, 5, 7, 9, 11, 13, and 15

From the assorted black-and-red prints, cut:
- 32 of piece A (page 102) for block corners
- 24 strips, 1⅞" x 8½", for sashing

From black-and-red print for inner and outer borders, cut from the lengthwise grain:
- 2 strips, 2½" x 38", for side inner-border strips
- 2 strips, 2½" x 42", for top and bottom inner-border strips
- 2 strips, 4½" x 44", for side outer-border strips
- 2 strips, 4½" x 53", for top and bottom outer-border strips

From the red print for middle border, cut:
- 5 strips, 1½" x 42"

From the fabric for binding, cut:
- 5 strips, 2" x 42"

BLOCK CONSTRUCTION

1. Make 32 copies of the Pickle Dish Arc foundation pattern on page 101.

2. Referring to "Blocks Made with Long Strips" on pages 17–18, paper piece 32 arcs. Use black tone-on-tone prints for pieces 1, 3, 5, 7, 9, 11, 13, and 15; and assorted red prints for pieces 2, 4, 6, 8, 10, 12, and 14.

Make 32.

3. Referring to "Joining Curved Units" on page 20, sew a piece A to each of the arcs.

Make 32.

4. Sew a 1⅞" red print square to each end of 16 of the arcs.

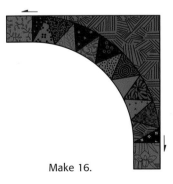

Make 16.

5. Sew a piece B to each of the remaining arcs.

Make 16.

6. Repeat step 5 to sew the arc from step 4 to each of the units from step 5.

Make 16.

Quilt-Top Assembly

1. Arrange and sew together the blocks, sashing, and sashing squares in horizontal rows. Rotate blocks as needed to form the design. Sew the rows together.

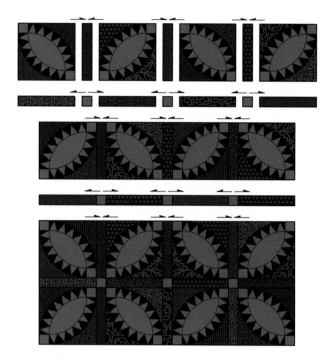

2. Referring to "Borders with Straight-Cut Corners" on pages 21–23, measure and trim the inner-border strips and sew them to the side edges of the quilt top first, and then to the top and bottom edges. Repeat for the middle border and outer border.

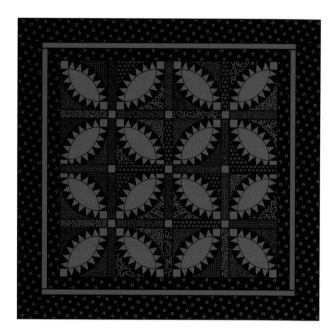

3. Layer the quilt top with batting and backing; baste. Quilt as desired. Bind the edges and add a sleeve, if desired. Add a label.

PEONY STAR

PEONY STAR *by Nancy Mahoney. Machine quilted by Lea Wang. Red and green fabrics complement the floral print in the border to make a holiday quilt. This quilt would be equally exciting in a different color combination. The open areas can be filled with lavish quilting.*

FINISHED QUILT SIZE: 44½" x 44½"
FINISHED BLOCK SIZE: 6" x 6"

MATERIALS

42"-wide fabric

- 2 yds. total assorted light prints for blocks
- 1 yd. total assorted green prints for blocks
- ⅜ yd. total assorted red prints for blocks
- ¼ yd. red print for inner border
- 1⅜ yds. floral print for blocks and outer border
- 2¾ yds. for backing
- 50" x 50" piece of batting
- ⅜ yd. for binding

CUTTING

CUT STRIPS ACROSS the width of the fabric unless otherwise indicated.

From assorted light prints, cut:

- 8 strips, 3½" x 42", for pieces 1, 3, 5, and 7 of unit B of Blazing Star blocks
- 20 of piece C (page 104) for corners of Blazing Star blocks
- 4 squares, 2¼" x 2¼"; ◻ 8 triangles for pieces 2 and 3 of Arrowhead blocks
- 4 squares, 4" x 4"; ◻ 8 triangles for pieces 5 and 6 of Arrowhead blocks
- 2 squares, 7½" x 7½"; ◻ 4 triangles for piece 7 of Arrowhead blocks
- 4 squares, 9¾" x 9¾"; ⊠ 16 triangles for side and corner setting triangles

From the assorted green prints, cut:

- 10 strips, 2½" x 42", for pieces 2, 4, and 6 of unit A and 2, 4, and 6 of unit B of Blazing Star blocks
- 2 squares, 4" x 4"; ◻ 4 triangles for piece 4 of Arrowhead blocks

From the assorted red prints, cut:

- 5 strips, 1¼" x 42", for pieces 1, 3, 5, and 7 of unit A of Blazing Star blocks
- 4 squares, 2¼" x 2¼", for piece 1 of Arrowhead blocks

From the red print for inner border, cut:

- 2 strips, 1½" x 36", for sides
- 2 strips, 1½" x 38", for top and bottom

From the floral print for outer border, cut from the lengthwise grain:

- 2 strips, 4½" x 38", for sides
- 2 strips, 4½" x 47", for top and bottom

From the fabric for binding, cut:

- 5 strips, 2" x 42"

BLOCK CONSTRUCTION

1. Make 20 copies each of unit A and unit B Blazing Star foundation patterns on page 103.

2. Referring to "Blocks Made with Long Strips" on pages 17–18, paper piece 20 of unit A. Use

red prints for pieces 1, 3, 5, and 7; use green prints for pieces 2, 4, and 6.

Unit A
Make 20.

3. Paper piece 20 of unit B. Use light prints for pieces 1, 3, 5, and 7; use green prints for pieces 2, 4, and 6.

Unit B
Make 20.

4. Referring to "Joining Curved Units" on page 20, sew unit A to unit B.

Match points.

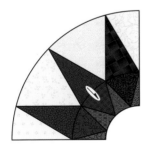

Make 20.

5. Sew a piece C to a unit from step 4.

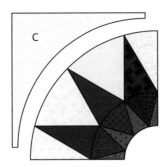

Make 20.

6. Sew 4 blocks together.

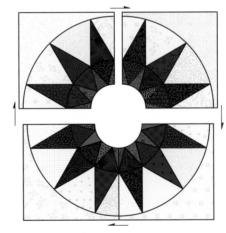

Make 5.

7. Make a paper circle of pattern D (page 104). Cut 5 of piece D from the floral print, adding a ¼" seam allowance all around. Pin the paper circle on the wrong side of the fabric. Make a running stitch ⅛" from the outside edge, and then pull the thread to gather. Arrange the gathers and press the edges. Remove the paper and appliqué a circle to the center of each block.

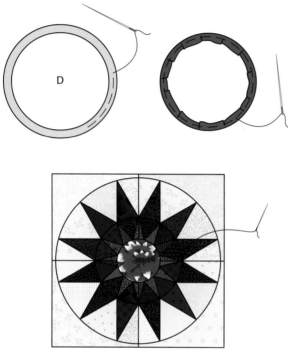

D

Make 5.

8. Make 4 copies of the Arrowhead foundation pattern on page 91.

9. Paper piece 4 Arrowhead blocks. Use a red square for piece 1; use assorted light prints for pieces 2, 3, 5, 6, and 7; use a green print for piece 4.

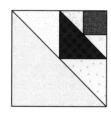

Make 4.

10. Sew 2 side setting triangles to the sides of the Arrowhead blocks to make a large side setting unit.

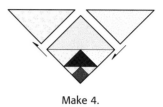

Make 4.

QUILT-TOP ASSEMBLY

1. Arrange the Blazing Star blocks and side setting units in diagonal rows. Sew 2 triangles together to make each of the 4 corner setting triangles. Sew the rows together, adding the corner setting triangles last.

2. Referring to "Borders with Straight-Cut Corners" on pages 21–23, measure and trim the inner-border strips and sew them to the side edges of the quilt top first, and then to the top and bottom edges. Repeat for the outer border.

3. Layer the quilt top with batting and backing; baste. Quilt as desired. Bind the edges and add a sleeve, if desired. Add a label.

Tequila Sunrise

Tequila Sunrise *by Nancy Mahoney. Machine quilted by Lea Wang. The pieced border looks complicated, but it is easy to accomplish with paper piecing, and it sets off the center medallion dramatically. The red fabrics glow on the light background but would be equally effective with a dark background.*

Finished quilt size: 55½" x 55½"
Finished block size: 6" x 6"

MATERIALS

42"-wide fabric

- 2¾ yds. total assorted light prints for blocks
- 1⅞ yds. total assorted red prints for blocks and sashing squares
- 1½ yds. light print for sashing, setting triangles, and inner border
- 1¾ yds. red print for outer border
- 3½ yds. for backing
- 61" x 61" piece of batting
- ⅜ yd. for binding

CUTTING

CUT STRIPS ACROSS the width of the fabric unless otherwise indicated.

From the assorted light prints, cut:
- 24 of piece F (page 105) for outside corner of New York Beauty blocks
- 17 strips, 2¼" x 42", for pieces 1, 3, 5, 7, 9, 11, and 13 of New York Beauty blocks and pieces 2 and 3 of corner blocks
- 20 strips, 1½" x 42", for pieces 1, 3, 5, 7, 9, 11, and 13 of border blocks

From the assorted red prints, cut:
- 32 strips, 1½" x 42", for pieces 2, 4, 6, 8, 10, and 12 of New York Beauty blocks; pieces 2, 4, 6, 8, 10, and 12 of border blocks; and piece 1 of corner blocks
- 24 of piece E (page 105) for inside corner of New York Beauty blocks
- 5 squares, 2" x 2", for sashing squares

From the light print for sashing, setting triangles, and inner border, cut from the lengthwise grain:
- 2 strips, 2" x 45", for sashing
- 2 strips, 1⅜" x 42", for side inner-border strips
- 2 strips, 1⅜" x 44", for top and bottom inner-border strips

From the remaining fabric, cut:
- 20 strips, 2" x 6½", for sashing
- 6 strips, 2" x 14", for sashing
- 2 squares, 9¾" x 9¾"; ⊠ 8 side setting triangles
- 2 squares, 10½" x 10½"; ◻ 4 corner setting triangles

From the red print for outer border, cut from the lengthwise grain:
- 2 strips, 4½" x 48", for sides
- 2 strips, 4½" x 57", for top and bottom

From the fabric for binding, cut:
- 6 strips, 2" x 42"

BLOCK CONSTRUCTION

1. Make 24 copies of the New York Beauty "teeth" foundation pattern on page 106.

2. Referring to "Blocks Made with Long Strips" on pages 17–18, paper piece 24 teeth units. Start with a light print for piece 1. Use the 1½"-wide red strips for pieces 2, 4, 6, 8, 10, and 12; and the 2¼"-wide light-print strips for pieces 3, 5, 7, 9, 11 and 13.

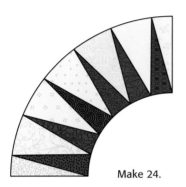

Make 24.

3. Referring to "Joining Curved Units" on page 20, sew a piece E to each of the teeth units.

Make 24.

4. Sew a piece F to each of the units from step 3.

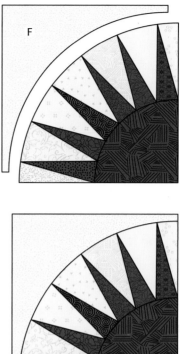

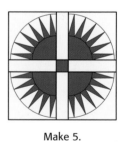

Make 24.

5. Join 4 blocks, four 2" x 6½" light sashing pieces, and one 2" red square to make a large block.

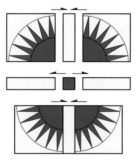

Make 5.

6. Make 28 copies of the border-block foundation pattern on page 107.

7. Paper piece 28 border blocks. Start with a light print for piece 1. Use the 1½"-wide red strips for pieces 2, 4, 6, 8, 10, and 12; use the 1½"-wide light-print strips for pieces 3, 5, 7, 9, 11, and 13.

Make 28.

8. Make 4 copies of the corner-block foundation pattern on page 107.

9. Paper piece 4 corner blocks. Use a red print for piece 1 and light prints for pieces 2 and 3.

Make 4.

10. Sew 2 side setting triangles to the New York Beauty blocks to make large side setting units.

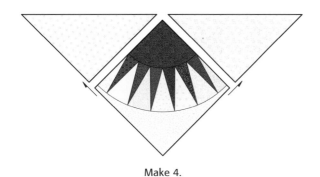

Make 4.

QUILT-TOP ASSEMBLY

1. Arrange the large blocks, sashing, and side-setting units in diagonal rows. Sew the units together in diagonal rows. Sew the rows together with sashing between the rows, adding the corner setting triangles last.

2. Trim the sides of the quilt top to straighten the edges.

3. Referring to "Borders with Straight-Cut Corners" on pages 21–23, measure and trim the inner-border strips and sew them to the side edges of the quilt top first, and then to the top and bottom edges.

NOTE: *After you add the inner border, the quilt top must measure 42½" x 42½" (including seam allowances) for the pieced border to fit properly. Adjust the width of the inner border if necessary to achieve the correct size.*

4. Join 7 border blocks to make each of 4 pieced-border strips.

5. Sew 1 pieced-border strip to each side edge, placing the light triangles toward the center of the quilt top. Sew a corner block to each end of the remaining pieced-border strips and then sew the strips to the top and bottom edges.

6. Measure, trim, and sew the red outer-border strips as for inner border.

7. Layer the quilt top with batting and backing; baste. Quilt as desired. Bind the edges and add a sleeve, if desired. Add a label.

Patterns

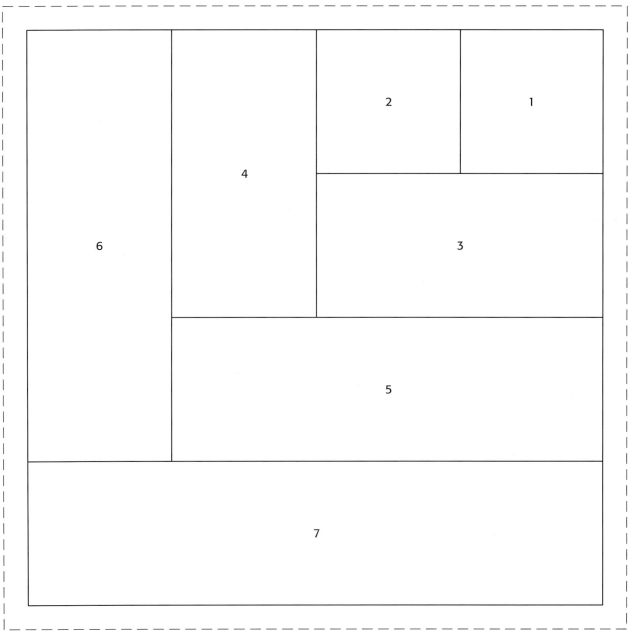

Quarter Log Cabin

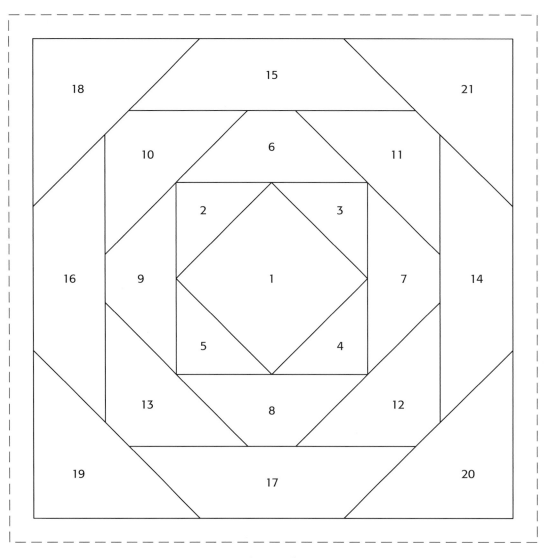

Pineapple

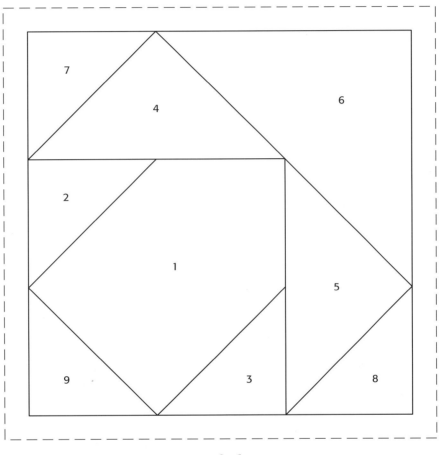

T Block

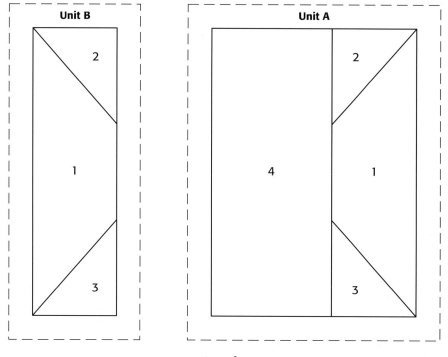

Spools

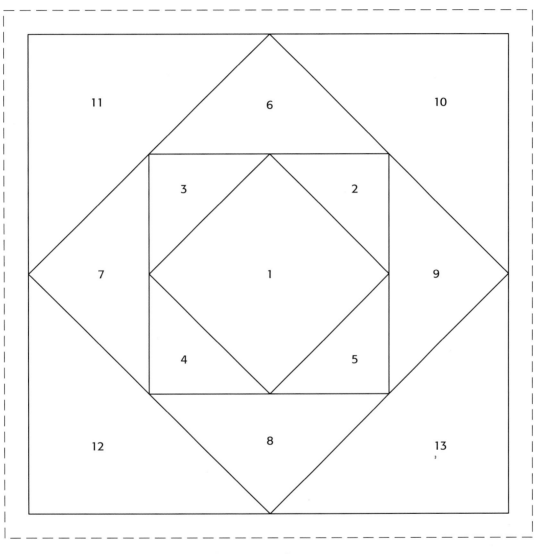

Square-on-Square

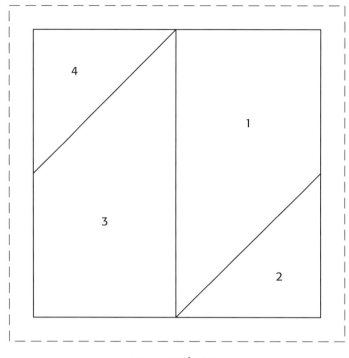

Four-Patch Star

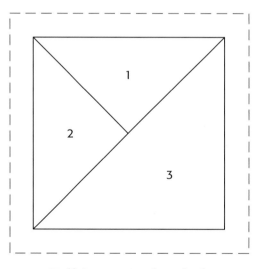

Half-Square Border Block

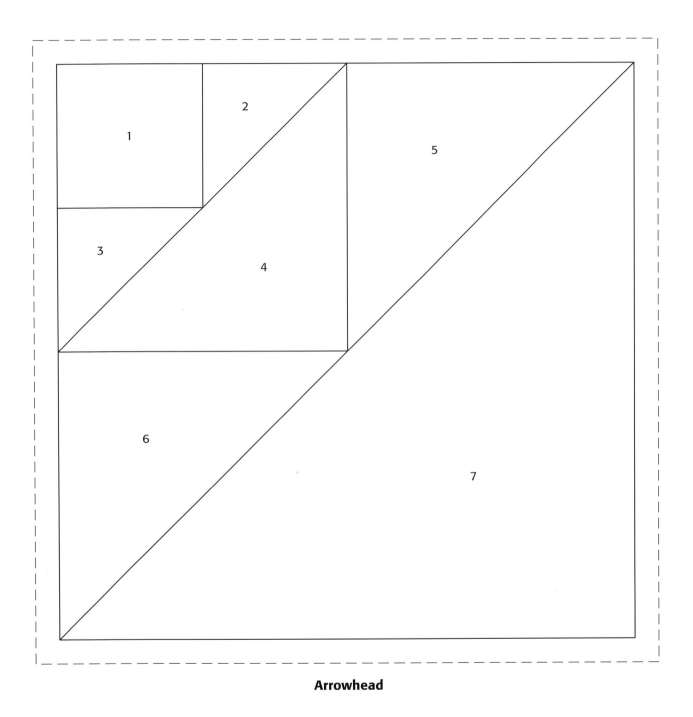

Arrowhead

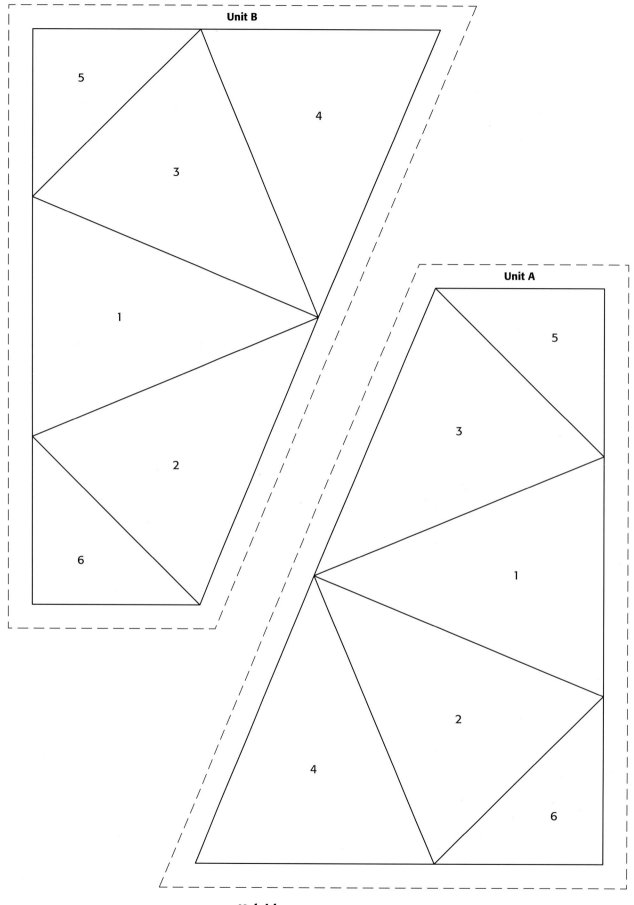

Unit B

5

4

3

1

2

6

Unit A

5

3

1

2

4

6

Kaleidoscope

Unit A

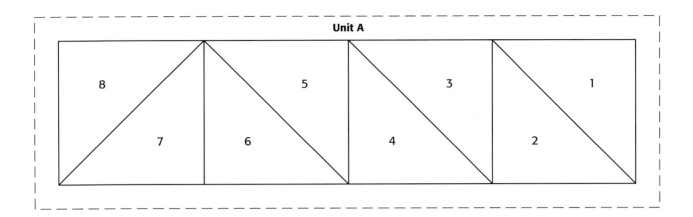

Unit B

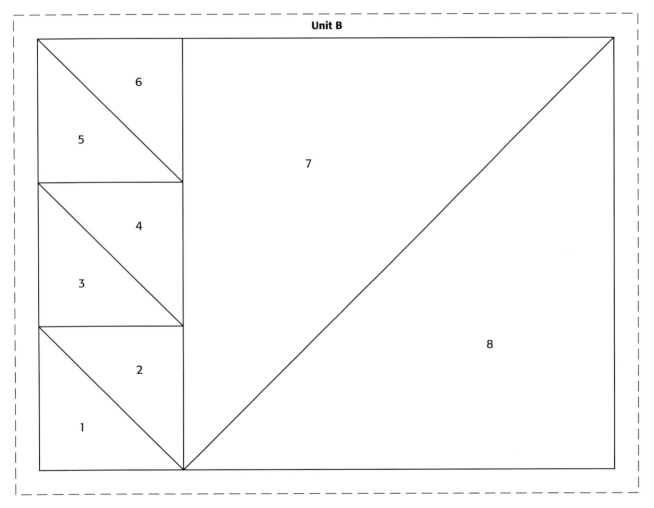

Delectable Mountain

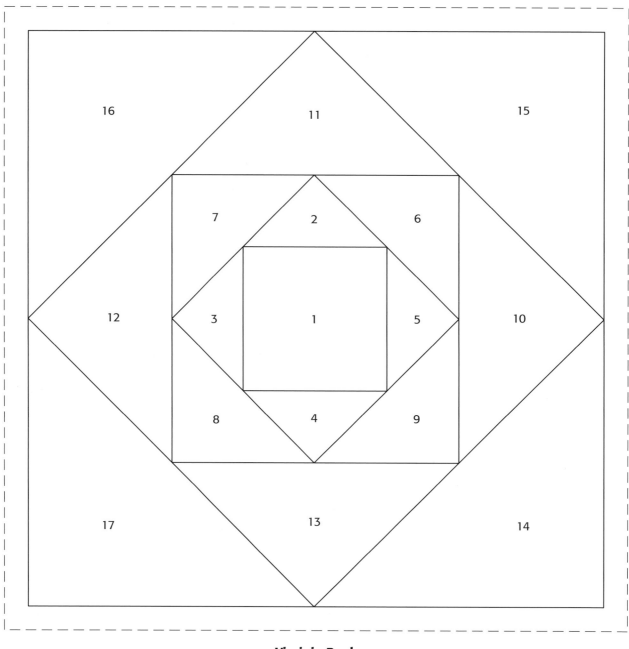

Virginia Reel

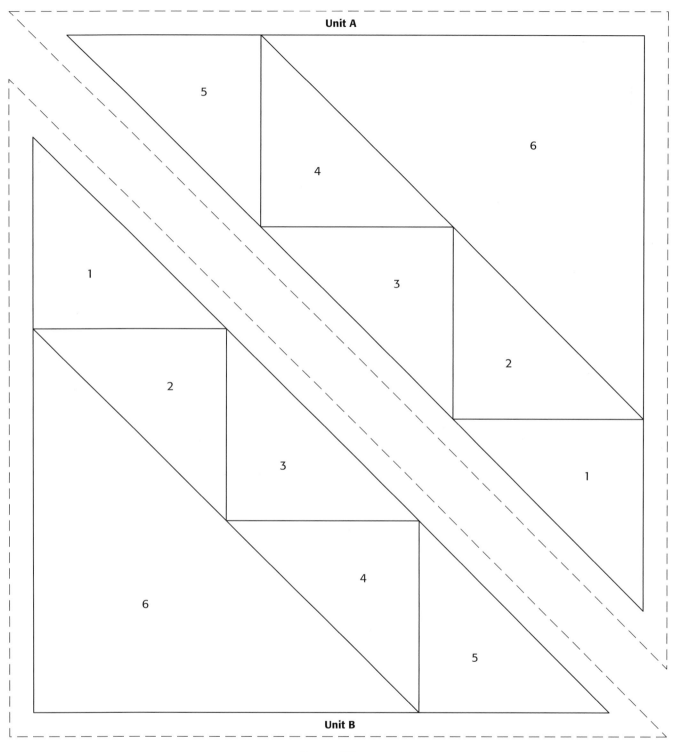

Ocean Waves

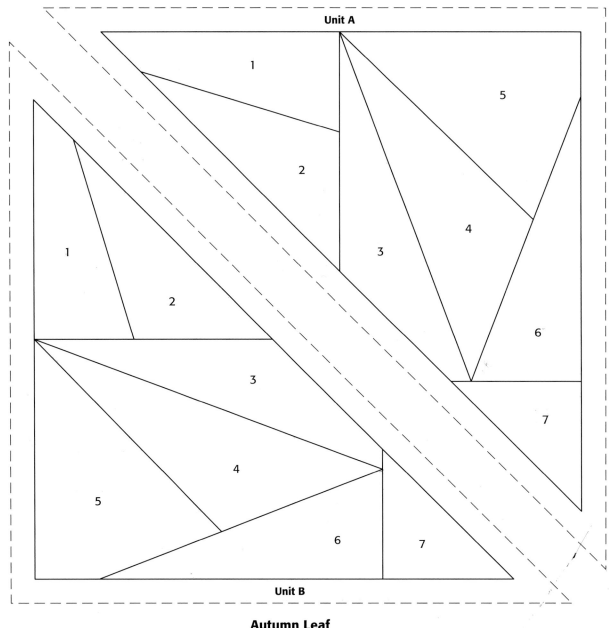

**Autumn Leaf
5" Block**

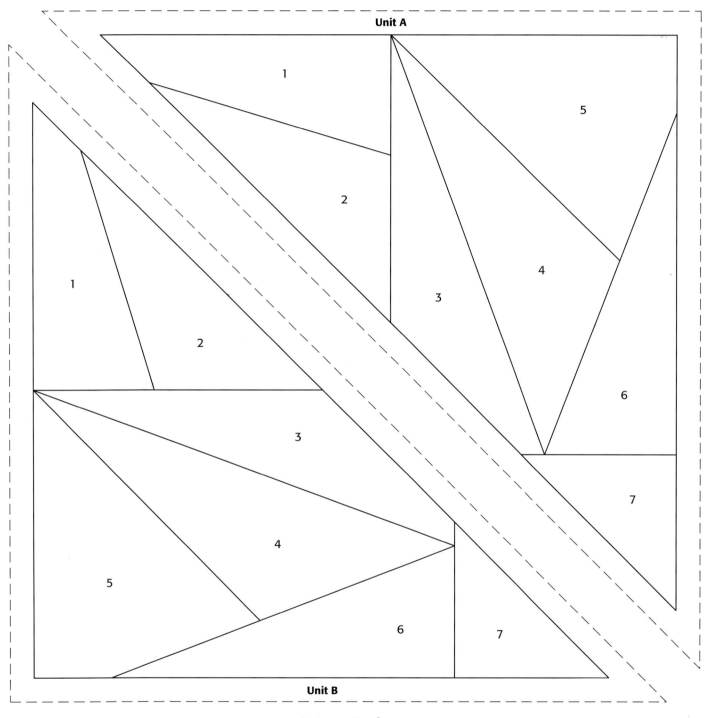

Unit A

Unit B

Autumn Leaf
6" Block

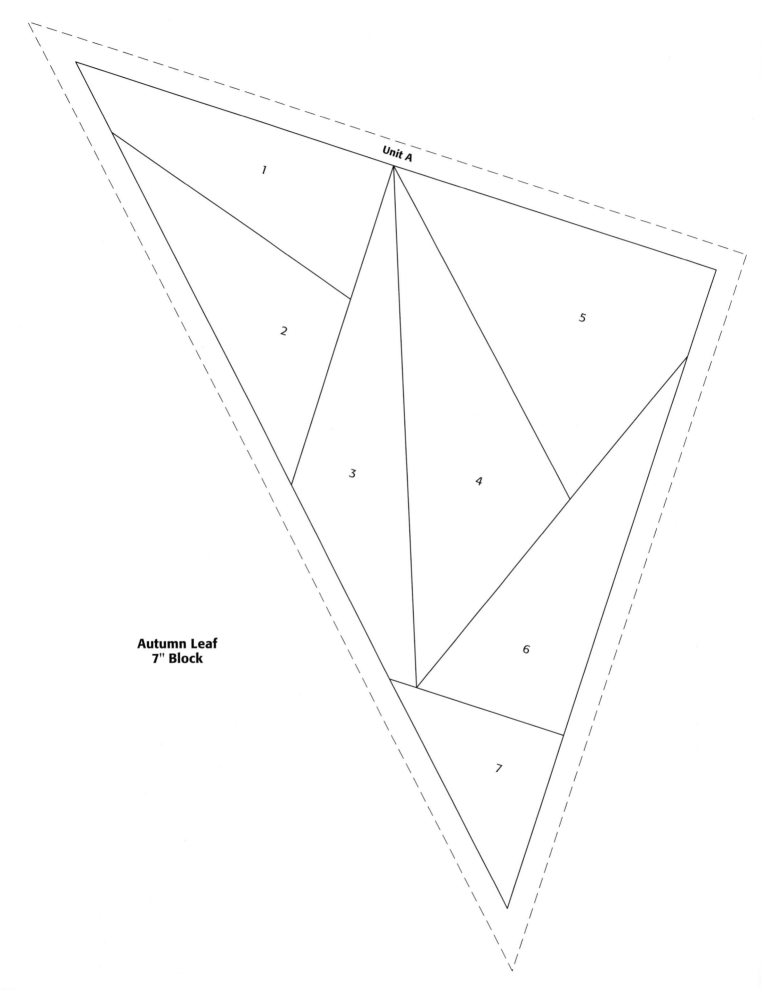

Unit A

1

2

3

4

5

6

7

Autumn Leaf
7" Block

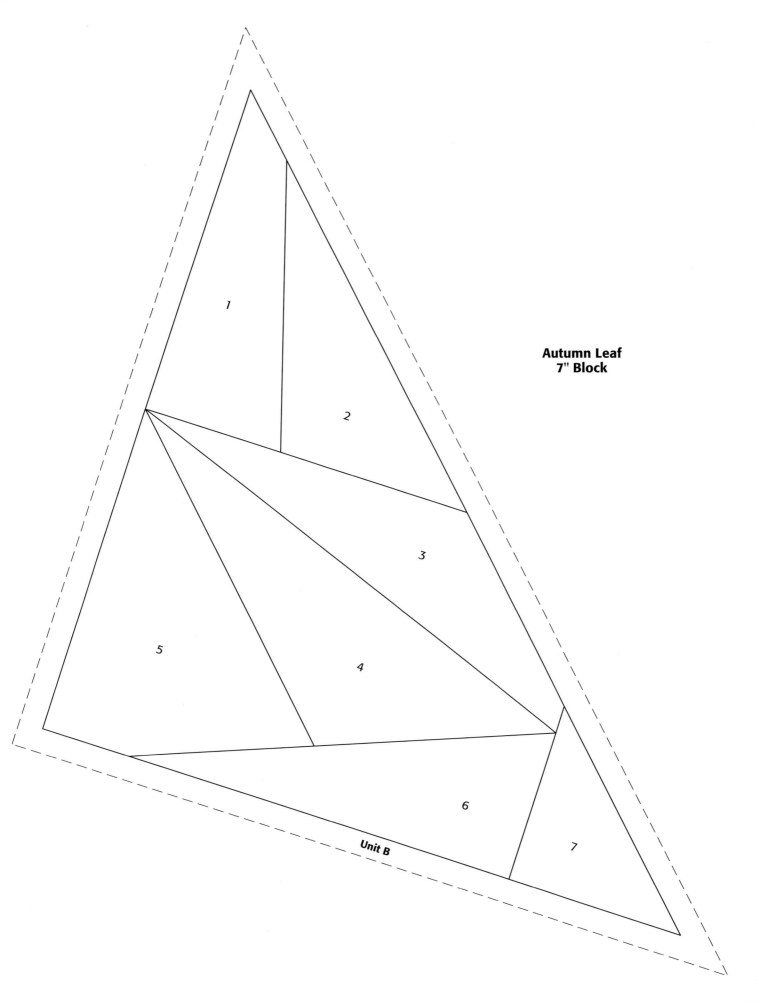

**Autumn Leaf
7" Block**

1

2

3

5

4

6

7

Unit B

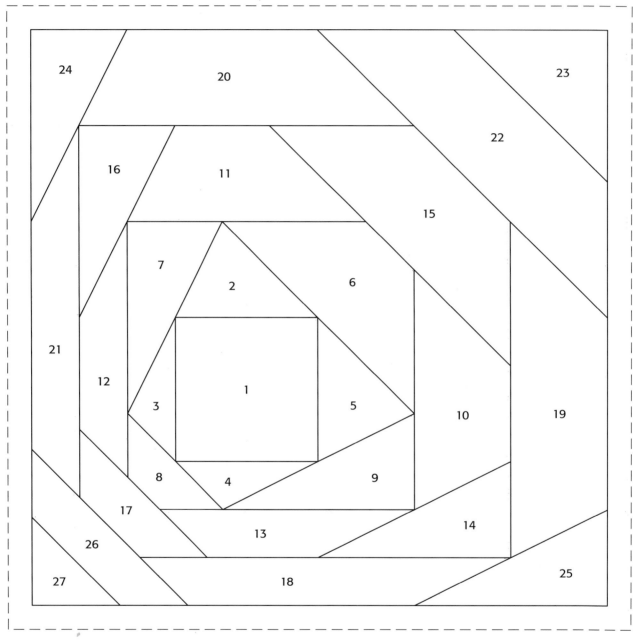

Off-Center Pineapple

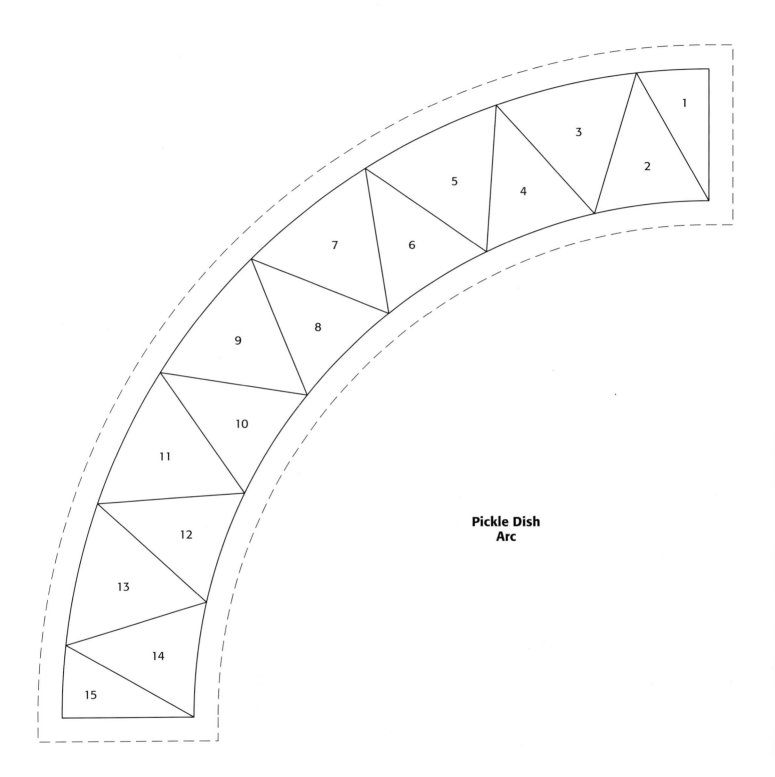

**Pickle Dish
Arc**

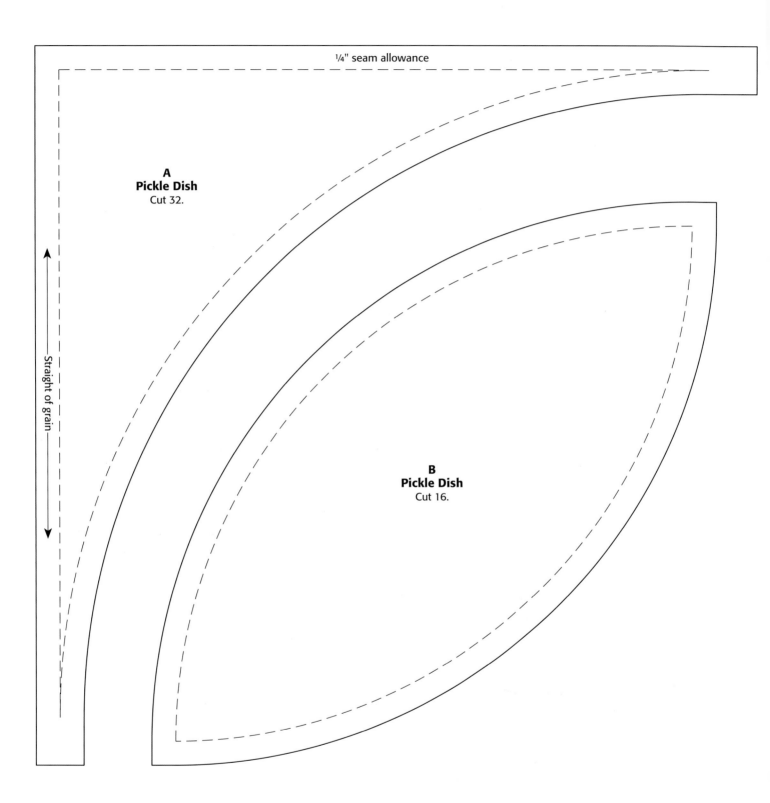

¼" seam allowance

A
Pickle Dish
Cut 32.

Straight of grain

B
Pickle Dish
Cut 16.

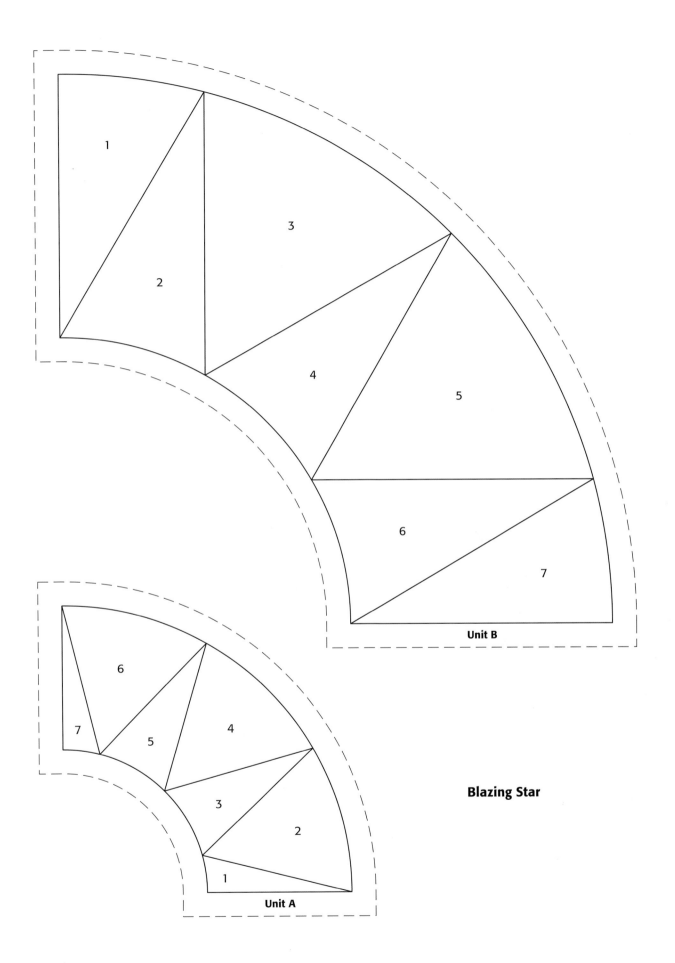

Blazing Star

Unit A

Unit B

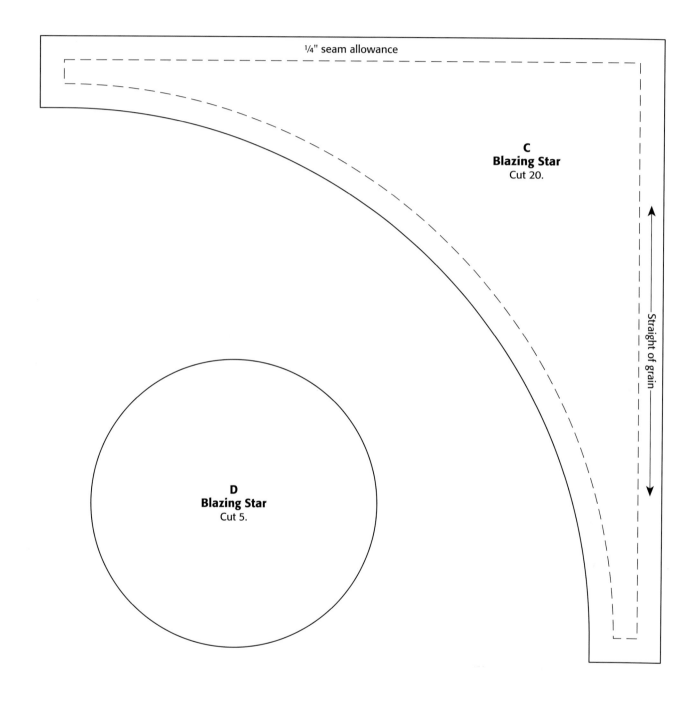

¼" seam allowance

C
Blazing Star
Cut 20.

Straight of grain

D
Blazing Star
Cut 5.

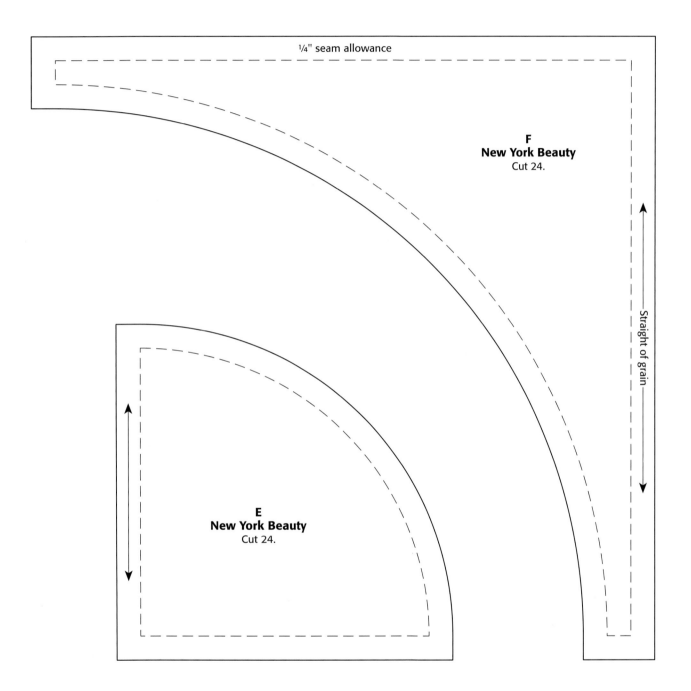

¼" seam allowance

F
New York Beauty
Cut 24.

Straight of grain

E
New York Beauty
Cut 24.

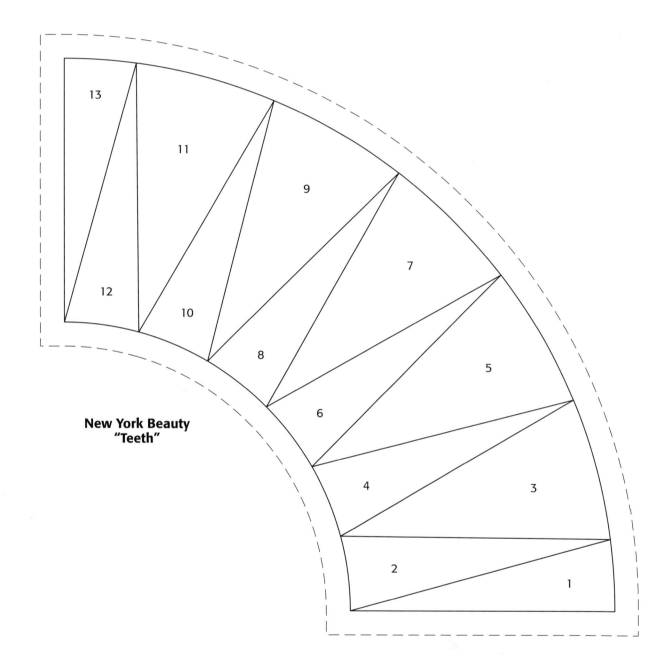

New York Beauty
"Teeth"

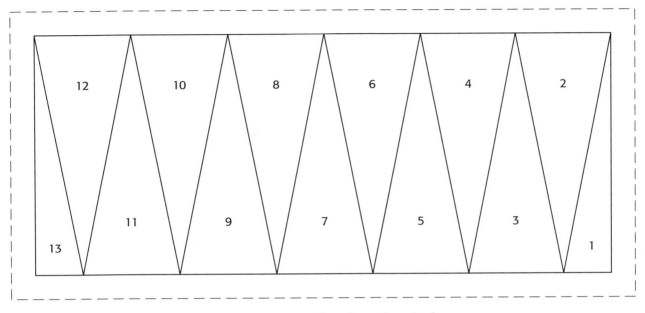

Tequila Sunrise Pieced-Border Block

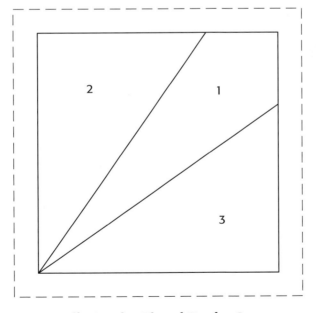

Tequila Sunrise Pieced-Border Corner

RESOURCES

THE FOLLOWING RESOURCES sell fat quarters and/or cut squares. Contact each resource directly for availability.

COTTON CLUB
PO Box 2263
Boise, ID 83701
208-345-5567
www.cottonclub.com

CONNECTING THREADS
13118 NE 4th Street
Vancouver, WA 98684
800-574-6454
www.connectingthreads.com

HANCOCK'S OF PADUCAH
3841 Hinkleville Rd
Paducah, KY 42001
800-845-8723
www.hancocks-paducah.com

KEEPSAKE QUILTING
Route 25B - PO Box 1618
Center Harbor, NH 03226
800-525-8086
www.keepsakequilting.com

ABOUT THE AUTHOR

Nancy Mahoney's love for scrap quilts began at the age of seven, when she made a one-patch pillow top from scraps. While growing up, Nancy would put the family Double Wedding Ring quilt made from scraps on her bed whenever possible. The quilt was made by Catherine Ellen Fowler Clark Carty, Nancy's maternal great-grandmother, and it is now part of Nancy's collection of vintage quilts, although a little worn from much use and love.

Nancy began quilting in earnest in 1987. Several of her quilts have been featured in books and national quilt magazines. Her quilts have been juried into the AQS quilt show in Paducah, Kentucky, and the APNQ Quilt Show in Seattle, Washington. Nancy's quilts have also won many awards, including two first-place ribbons.

When Nancy is not quilting, she enjoys gardening, reading, and shopping for antiques.

I'm glad I never threw them away;
my scraps of yore are my quilts today.

—SANDRA L. O'BRIEN
Great American Quilts, 1988

new and bestselling titles from

America's Best-Loved Craft & Hobby Books™

America's Best-Loved Quilt Books®

NEW RELEASES
Bear's Paw Plus
All Through the Woods
American Quilt Classics
Amish Wall Quilts
Animal Kingdom CD-ROM
Batik Beauties
The Casual Quilter
Fantasy Floral Quilts
Fast Fusible Quilts
Friendship Blocks
From the Heart
Log Cabin Fever
Machine-Stitched Cathedral Stars
Magical Hexagons
Quilts From Larkspur Farm
Potting Shed Patchwork
Repliqué Quilts
Successful Scrap Quilts
   From Simple Rectangles

APPLIQUÉ
Artful Album Quilts
Artful Appliqué
Colonial Appliqué
Red and Green: An Appliqué Tradition
Rose Sampler Supreme

BABY QUILTS
Easy Paper-Pieced Baby Quilts
Even More Quilts for Baby: Easy as ABC
More Quilts for Baby: Easy as ABC
Play Quilts
The Quilted Nursery
Quilts for Baby: Easy as ABC

HOLIDAY QUILTS
Christmas at That Patchwork Place
Holiday Collage Quilts
Paper Piece a Merry Christmas
A Snowman's Family Album Quilt
Welcome to the North Pole

LEARNING TO QUILT
Basic Quiltmaking Techniques for:
   Borders and Bindings
   Divided Circles
   Hand Appliqué
   Machine Appliqué
   Strip Piecing
The Joy of Quilting
The Simple Joys of Quilting
Your First Quilt Book (or it should be!)

PAPER PIECING
50 Fabulous Paper-Pieced Stars
For the Birds
Paper Piece a Flower Garden
Paper-Pieced Bed Quilts
Paper-Pieced Curves
A Quilter's Ark
Show Me How to Paper Piece

ROTARY CUTTING
101 Fabulous Rotary-Cut Quilts
365 Quilt Blocks a Year Perpetual Calendar
Around the Block Again
Biblical Blocks
Creating Quilts with Simple Shapes
Flannel Quilts
More Fat Quarter Quilts
More Quick Watercolor Quilts
Razzle Dazzle Quilts

SCRAP QUILTS
Nickel Quilts
Scrap Frenzy
Scrappy Duos
Spectacular Scraps

CRAFTS
The Art of Stenciling
Baby Dolls and Their Clothes
Creating with Paint
The Decorated Kitchen
The Decorated Porch
A Handcrafted Christmas
Painted Chairs
Sassy Cats

KNITTING & CROCHET
Too Cute!
Clever Knits
Crochet for Babies and Toddlers
Crocheted Sweaters
Fair Isle Sweaters Simplified
Irresistible Knits
Knit It Your Way
Knitted Shawls, Stoles, and Scarves
Knitted Sweaters for Every Season
Knitting with Novelty Yarns
Paintbox Knits
Simply Beautiful Sweaters
Simply Beautiful Sweaters for Men
The Ultimate Knitter's Guide

Our books are available at bookstores and your favorite craft, fabric and yarn retailers. If you don't see the title you're looking for, visit us at www.martingale-pub.com or contact us at:

1-800-426-3126

International: 1-425-483-3313

Fax: 1-425-486-7596

E-mail: info@martingale-pub.com

For more information and a full list of our titles, visit our Web site or call for a free catalog.

1/02